ABOUT THE AUTHOR

LEO TOLSTOY (1828–1910) is the author of *War and Peace* (1869), *Anna Karenina* (1877), *The Death of Ivan Ilyich* (1886), *Family Happiness* (1859), and other classics of Russian literature.

ABOUT THE TRANSLATOR

DUSTIN CONDREN received an MA and ABD in Slavic languages and literatures from Stanford University. His recent translations include Anton Chekhov's short dramatic works, which have been performed in theaters in New York City and San Diego. He lives and works as a translator and language instructor in Brooklyn, New York.

THE GOSPEL IN BRIEF

The Gospel *in* Brief

THE LIFE OF JESUS

Leo Tolstoy

TRANSLATED BY

Dustin Condren

HARPER PERENNIAL

NEW YORK • LONDON • TORONTO • SYDNEY • NEW DELHI • AUCKLAND

HARPER ● PERENNIAL

HarperCollins books may be purchased for educational, business, or sales promotional use. For information, please e-mail the Special Markets Department at SPsales@harpercollins.com.

FIRST EDITION

Designed by Fritz Metsch

Library of Congress Cataloging-in-Publication Data in available upon request.

ISBN 978-0-06-199345-9

24 25 26 27 28 LBC 19 18 17 16 15

CONTENTS

THE GOSPEL
A Proclamation on Goodness from Jesus Christ, the Son of God

FOREWORD

Toward the end of an exceptionally fruitful period of fiction writing in the 1860s and 1870s, in which he produced such enduring classics as *War and Peace* and *Anna Karenina*, Leo Tolstoy was shaken by a personal and spiritual crisis that effectively halted his labors as a novelist. He had fallen into despair, become preoccupied with death and found himself on the verge of suicide, navigating existence with nothing more than the nihilistic belief that he was "an accidental clutter of parts, that there was no purpose in life and that life itself is evil." In this deep existential anguish, Tolstoy recalled the Christianity he had seen in his youth and located some hope in the memory of the simple believers among whom he had grown up. He saw in these believers an example of a real, fulfilled life, and it was this recollection that encouraged him to begin a deep study of the Christian teaching as found in the Gospel. This spiritual crisis and its consequences are documented in detail in Tolstoy's subsequent nonfiction work, serving as the impetus for his texts on personal spirituality, such as *A Confession*, *What I Believe* and *The Kingdom of God Is Within You*.

Tolstoy's study of the Bible, which he began in 1879 purely for personal enlightenment, had developed by the following year into a massive project in which he intended to retranslate the four books of the Gospel and synthesize them into one narrative. This labor, which lasted for close to three years, was transformative. He would later refer to it as a time of intense concentration and "constant, rapturous exertion of my soul." He felt that he had "come to know the light" and, in the words of his wife, Sofia Andreyevna, this study had made the normally stentorian Tolstoy "calm, concentrated and quiet."

A large portion of his study was devoted to referencing early Greek texts with the help of books by the biblical scholars Johan Griesbach, Constantin von Tischendorff, Édouard Reuss and Vasilii Grechulevich, as well as checking the Latin Vulgate and certain German, French, and English translations of the Gospels. Tolstoy also frequently made use of his philologist friend and tutor to the Tolstoy children, I. M. Ivakin, who was readily available on the estate at Yasnaya Polyana. He set upon the texts vigorously, dismissing any reservations about the spiritual sanctity of the words themselves, or his theological qualification for such work, asserting with some humor that the most remarkable aspect of this translation process was that "an artillery lieutenant had decided to translate a Greek book for himself."

The purpose of Tolstoy's investigation into the Christian Gospel was to find the practical, pure teaching of Jesus Christ, to free it from the linguistic patina of ritual and scripture, removing both the dogmatic and the supernatural. In illustration of this approach, Ivakin recalls an 1881 conversation in which Tolstoy said to him: "What is it to me if [Christ] was resurrected? If he was resurrected, then God bless him! The questions important to me are: What should I do? How should I live?"

The project, and indeed the direction of his own spiritual development, seems to have crystallized with the triumph he felt in translating the first ten verses of the Gospel of John, where he renders the familiar "In the beginning was the Word" as "As the basis and source of all things stood the knowledge of life." He felt that his usage of "knowledge of life" for "the Word" could be justified philologically, and this gambit seems to typify Tolstoy's approach to the text as a whole: He stretches the words themselves, ridding them of their encrusted ecclesiastical connotation, in order to reveal a text that corresponds to the deeper spiritual truth that he felt he had discovered in the course of his study.

Such stretching of the Bible verses is especially apparent in the accounts of Jesus's miracles. For Tolstoy, the miraculous multiplication of fishes and loaves becomes a lesson in communal sharing as his followers each learn to give away their food to others, the story of the healed blind man now operates as a slight metaphor in which restored sight is read as a type of spiritual "enlightenment," and Jesus's early temptation in the wilderness plays as a sort of Socratic dialogue with himself.

This labor to infuse the text with greater flexibility comes out more successfully—or more believably—in certain sections than it does in others. Ivakin felt that in many places Tolstoy had stretched things too far in order to support his previously held views, as did Tolstoy's great confidant and reader Nikolai Strakhov, who, though he supported the work as a whole, saw in his friend's translation "many weak spots and exaggerations" and took particular exception to his treatment of the first ten verses of the Gospel of John. Readers may also question the consistency of Tolstoy's translation at certain points. For example, he includes the episode of Jesus's conversation with the Samaritan woman at the well in chapter two and then repeats it without explanation in chapter five, using markedly different wording and emphasizing somewhat different aspects of the story.

Indeed, before long, Tolstoy began to feel the weakness of his philological justifications and admitted that in some places he had stretched meanings further than the original text could sustain. "There are many such places where . . . the sense is stretched and the translation is contrived. This happened because I wanted, as much as possible, to depolarize, as does a magnet, these words which had been given an entirely nonnative polarity as they have undergone interpretation by the church. To correct that alone would be a beneficial endeavor." And yet, despite admitting that he had overtaxed the Gospel words, it is clear that Tolstoy felt that his zeal was justified by his goal. His critical feeling toward the weakness of his philological arguments did not make him any less confident in the rightness of his understanding of the essential Christian teaching, a conviction that would carry him through the three years of his work on the Gospel.

By March 1881 he had produced a draft, in manuscript, of his translation, though he still felt that it was far from being ready to be published. It was titled *A Synthesis and Translation of the Four Gospels*. This work consisted of four distinct parts: an account of his personal spiritual life, his recent attraction to the Christian teaching, and how he came to understand it in his own terms; a discourse on and refutation of the Christian teaching as it had been falsely presented by the church; an investigation into the original teachings of Jesus, as found in the Gospel, and its synthesis into one narrative; and an interpretation of this text, an illumination of its true meaning, and a suggestion of the consequences that follow its teaching.

While the manuscript was in this form, V. I. Alekseyev, who had been staying on the estate as teacher to Tolstoy's eldest son, asked permission to make a copy of Tolstoy's text before his departure. Tolstoy consented, but as Alekseyev began his copying he realized that he would only have time for a portion of the work, and decided to copy out the third section where the actual synthesis and translation was located, omitting the other sections as well as all of the philological evidences that Tolstoy had labored over to justify his decisions as translator. Tolstoy examined this copy and approved it, realizing how much he liked the compactness of this shorter account. Shortly afterward, he edited this version of the work, wrote a long preface for it, and titled it *A Brief Account of the Gospel*. In a November 1881 letter to Strakhov he says that it would make a good small book and that he would like to see it published in the fall, but that it must be published abroad. Tolstoy felt some satisfaction with this condensed text and simultaneously felt so overwhelmed with the unwieldiness and seemingly infinite revisions required for the larger work that, apart from some minor adjusting here and there, he never returned in earnest to finish the project.

One need not read very far into the text to see just how inflammatory Tolstoy's translation would have been to the leadership of Orthodox Christianity. Not only was it a drastic rewording of sacred text, and therefore sacrilegious, but it went so far as to draw very direct parallels between the Orthodox leaders of the nineteenth century and the Pharisees of the Gospels by referring in many places to the Pharisees as "the orthodox" (*pravoslavnye*). The preface also made it clear that the translation is a challenge to those against whom he polemicizes, and that reading his new version of the Gospel would leave them two choices—either to choose the path of "humble repentance and renunciation" of the lies they use to hide the true Christian teaching or to persecute him for exposing these deceptions. At a time when state power was tied so closely to church power, Tolstoy could not have hoped to have such subversive writing pass censorship review, and made no effort himself to have the work published in Russia.

Accordingly, the text's first publication was in a French translation by Tolstoy's friend L. D. Urusov. This was an abridged version that appeared in the Paris journal *La Nouvelle Vague* in July 1883. Tolstoy was not satisfied by this version, considering it to be a perversion of his writing. This was followed in 1885 by an English translation in a collection called *Christ's Christianity*, which also included *What I Believe* and *A Confession*. This version was also heavily edited and included only the introduction and the chapter summaries, without the text from the Gospel verses themselves.

The first Russian-language edition was published in Geneva in 1890, but this was also abundant with mistakes, as it was printed from an uncorrected copy of the manuscript. As with most unpublishable works, many different manuscripts and lithographs of the text were in circulation in Russia, sometimes under the title "The New Gospel." The first publication in Russia of *A Brief Account of the Gospel* did not occur until after the 1905 revolution, following a slight relaxation in censorship. It appeared in various editions in 1906, 1911, 1913 and 1918.

Vladimir Chertkov, a devoted follower and publisher of Tolstoy, had established Free Age Press (*Svobodnoe slovo*) in Christchurch, England, where, in 1905, he published a more authoritative Russian-language edition of Tolstoy's Gospel. It contained an updated preface that Chertkov had requested from Tolstoy. The text was reorganized by Chertkov, who, in addition to making many editorial changes, placed the chapter summaries into one section at the end of the book, a major departure from the manuscript version. This edition was also missing the conclusion, which Tolstoy had based on the First Epistle of John.

The two main English-language translations still in publication today were completed by Isabel Hapgood and Aylmer Maude, both of whom seem to have based their translations on the Chertkov version of the Russian text, and thus have their translations structured similarly. These translations, done quite early in the twentieth century, feature a preface, twelve chapters without summaries, no conclusion, and an appendix with all of the chapter summaries combined at the end.

In this current translation, I have referred only to the text as it appears in the Soviet-era academic edition of Tolstoy's complete works in ninety volumes, published by the state publishing house Khudozhestvennaia literatura (GIKhL) and edited by N. N. Gusev. The twenty-fourth volume of this collection, published in 1957, contains the larger, unfinished work (*A Synthesis and Translation of the Four Gospels*) as well as the condensed *A Brief Account of the Gospel*. The version produced in that volume was printed from the only existing manuscript to have been edited and approved by the author himself, and avoids the errors that appear in the Chertkov edition and those translations based on it.

I have maintained the original structure of the text, with the preface, an introduction, twelve chapters containing both Tolstoy's summary and the main text based on the Gospel verses, and the conclusion based on the First Epistle of John. The only structural change I have made is to remove the verse structure, following the precedent of previous translations, in order to allow the text a more cohesive, informal and episodic style. This decision was made in keeping with Tolstoy's stated desire to depolarize the text and retell the verses with the simplest popular language, which is the broad goal of this new translation. (A "Verse Index" is included at the end of this edition, for those readers who wish to refer to the traditional verse numbers.) In agreement with Gusev's observation in his notes to the 1881 text that "Tolstoy apparently tried to write his new work so that it was above all else understandable to the working Russian people," I have made every attempt to present a translation that is both light enough to appeal to a general public but strong enough to transport the profound truths that Tolstoy encountered in his reading of the Gospel.

—*Dustin Condren*

PREFACE

This short account of the Gospel is my own synthesis of the four Gospels, organized according to the meaning of the teaching. While making this synthesis, it was mostly unnecessary for me to depart from the order in which the Gospels have already been laid out, so that in my synthesis one should not expect more but actually considerably fewer transpositions of Gospel verses than are found in the majority of concordances of which I am aware.

In the Gospel of John, as it appears in my synthesis, there are no transpositions whatsoever; it is all laid out in the exact order as the original.

The division of the Gospel into twelve or six chapters (if we were to count each thematic pair of two chapters as one) came about naturally from the meaning of the teaching.

This is the meaning behind these chapters:

1. Man is the son of an infinite source, the son of this father not by the flesh, but by the spirit.
2. And therefore man should serve this source in spirit.
3. The life of all people has a divine source. It alone is holy.
4. And therefore man should serve this source in the life of all people. That is the father's will.
5. Only serving the father's will can bring truth, i.e., a life of reason.

6. And therefore the satisfaction of one's own will is not necessary for true life.

7. Temporal, mortal life is the food of the true life—it is the material for a life of reason.

8. And therefore the true life is outside of time, it exists only in the present.

9. Life's deception with time: the life of the past or the future hides the true life of the present from people.

10. And therefore man should strive to destroy the deception of the temporal life of the past and the future.

11. The true life is not just life outside of time—the present—but is also a life outside of the individual. Life is common to all people and expresses itself in love.

12. And therefore, the person who lives in the present, in the common life of all people, unites himself with the father—with the source and foundation of life.

Each two chapters share a connection of effect and cause. Besides these twelve chapters, the following is appended to the account: the introduction from the first chapter of John, in which the writer speaks, on his own authority, about the meaning of the teaching as a whole, as well as the conclusion from the same writer's Epistle (written, likely, before the Gospel), containing some general conclusions on all that came before.

The introduction and conclusion do not represent an essential part of this teaching. They are simply general views on the teaching as a whole. Although the introduction and the conclusion both could have been omitted with no loss to the meaning of the teaching (especially since they were both written by John and do not come from Jesus), I held on to them for their simple and reasoned understanding of Jesus's teachings, and because these sections, unlike the church's strange interpretations, confirm one another and confirm the teaching as a whole while presenting the simplest articulation of meaning that could be attached to the teachings.

At the beginning of every chapter, apart from a short summary of its contents, I also present corresponding words from the prayer that Jesus used as a model to teach his students how to pray.

When I came to the completion of this work, I found, to my surprise and joy, that the so-called Lord's Prayer is nothing other than Jesus's whole teaching expressed in its most distilled form in the very order that I had already laid out the chapters, and that each expression in the prayer corresponds to the sense and order of the chapters.

1.	*Our father*	Man is the son of God.
2.	*Who art in heaven.*	God is the eternal, spiritual source of life.
3.	*Hallowed be thy name.*	Let this source of life be holy.
4.	*Thy kingdom come.*	Let his power be manifest in all people.
5.	*Thy will be done in heaven*	And let the eternal source's will come to be, both in and of itself
6.	*as it is on earth.*	as well as in the flesh.
7.	*Give us our daily bread*	Temporal life is the food of true life.
8.	*this day*	The true life is in the present.
9.	*And forgive us our debts, as we forgive our debtors.*	Let not the mistakes and delusions of the past hide the true life from us.

10.	*And lead us not into temptation.*	And let them not lead us into deception.
11.	*But deliver us from evil.*	And then there will be no evil.
12.	*For thine is the kingdom and the power and the glory.*	And it will be your power and strength and reason.

In the third section of the more comprehensive account, which is still in manuscript form, the Gospels according to the four Evangelists are thoroughly explicated, without the slightest omission. In this current account, the following verses are omitted: the conception, the birth of John the Baptist, his imprisonment and death, the birth of Jesus, his lineage, the flight with his mother into Egypt, Jesus's miracles in Canaan and Capernaum, the casting out of demons, walking on water, the withering of the fig tree, healing of the sick, the resurrection of the dead, Christ's own resurrection and all references to prophecies fulfilled in Christ's life.

These verses are omitted in the current short account because, since they do not contain any teaching but only describe events that occurred before, during or after Jesus's ministry without adding anything, they only complicate and burden the account. These verses, no matter how they are understood, do not contain contradictions to the teaching, nor do they contain support for it. The only value these verses held for Christianity was that they proved the divinity of Jesus to those who did not believe in it. For someone who perceives the flimsiness of a story about miracles, but still does not doubt Jesus's divinity because of the strength of his teaching, these verses fall away by themselves; they are unnecessary.

In the larger account, each departure from the standard translation, each interjected clarification, each omission is explained and justified by a collation of the different versions of the Gospel, contexts, philological and other considerations. In this short account,

all of these proofs and refutations of the church's false understand-
ings, as well as the detailed annotations with references, have been
left out on the basis that no matter how exact and correct the reasoning of each individual section may be, such reasoning cannot
serve to convince anyone that this reading of the teaching is true.
The proof that this reading is correct lies not in reasoning out separate passages, but in the unity, clarity, simplicity and fullness of the
teaching itself and on its correspondence with the internal feelings
of every person who seeks truth.

Concerning all general deviations in my account from the accepted church texts, the reader should not forget that our quite customary concept about how the Gospels, all four, with all of their
verses and letters are essentially holy books is, from one perspective, the most vulgar delusion, and from the other perspective, the
most vulgar and harmful deception. The reader should understand
that at no point did Jesus himself ever write a book as did Plato,
Philo or Marcus Aurelius, that he did not even present his teachings
to literate and educated people, as Socrates did, but spoke with the
illiterate whom he met in the course of daily life, and that only long
after his death did it occur to people that what he had said was very
important and that it really wouldn't be a bad idea to write down
a little of what he had said and done, and so almost one hundred
years later they began to write down what they had heard about
him. The reader should remember that such writings were very,
very numerous, that many were lost, many were very bad, and
that the Christians used all of them before little by little picking
out the ones that seemed to them best and most sensible, and that
in choosing these best Gospels, to refer to the adage "every branch
has its knots," the churches inevitably took in a lot of knots with
what they had cut out from the entire massive body of literature on
Christ. There are many passages in the canonical Gospels that are
as bad as those in the rejected apocryphal ones, and many places in

the apocryphal ones are good. The reader should remember that Christ's teaching may be holy, but that there is no way for some set number of verses and letters to be holy, and that no book can be holy from its first line to its last simply because people say that it is holy. Of all educated people, only our Russian reader, thanks to Russia's censorship, can ignore the last one hundred years of labor by historical critics and continue to speak naively about how the Gospels of Matthew, Mark and Luke, as we currently have them, were each written completely and independently by the respective Evangelist. The reader should remember that to make this claim in the year 1880, ignoring all that has been developed on this subject by science, is the same as it would have been to say last century that the sun orbits the earth. The reader should remember that the Synoptic Gospels, as they have come down to us, are the fruit of a slow accumulation of elisions, ascriptions and the imaginations of thousands of different human minds and hands, and in no way a work of revelation directly from the Holy Ghost to the Evangelists. Remember that the attribution of the Gospels to the apostles is a fable that not only does not stand up to criticism, but has no foundation whatsoever, other than the desire of devout people that it were so. The Gospels were selected, added to, and interpreted over the centuries; all of the Gospels that have come down to us from the fourth century are written in continuous script, without punctuation. Since the fourth and fifth century they have been subject to the most varied readings, and such variants of the books of the Gospel can be numbered as high as fifty thousand. All of this should remind the reader not to become blinded by the customary view, that the Gospels, as they are now understood, came to us exactly as they are from the Holy Ghost. The reader should remember that not only is there no harm in throwing out the unnecessary parts of the Gospels and illuminating some passages with others, but that, on the contrary, it is reprehensible and godless not to do that, and continue considering some fixed number of verses and letters to be holy.

Only people who do not seek for truth and do not love the teachings of Christ can maintain such a view of the Gospels.

On the other hand, I ask the reader of my account of the Gospels to remember that if I do not look at the Gospels as holy books that come to us from heaven via the Holy Ghost, I also do not look at the Gospels as if they were merely major works in the history of religious literature. I understand both the divine and the secular view of the Gospels, but I view them differently. Therefore I ask the reader, while reading my account, not to fall into either the church's view or the historical view of the Gospel customary to educated people in recent times, which I did not hold and which I also find incomplete. I do not look at *Christianity* as a strictly divine revelation, nor as a historical phenomenon, but I look at *Christianity* as a teaching that gives meaning to life. I was brought to Christianity neither by theological nor historical investigations, but by the fact that fifty years after my birth, having asked myself and all the wise ones in my circle who I am and what the purpose of my life is, I received the answer that I am an accidental clutter of parts, that there is no purpose in life and that life itself is evil. I was brought to Christianity because having received such an answer, I fell into despair and wanted to kill myself; but remembering that before, in childhood, when I believed, there had been a purpose to my life and that the believers who surrounded me—the majority of whom were uncorrupted by riches—lived a real life. I began to doubt the veracity of the answer that had been given to me via the wisdom of the people in my circle and I attempted to understand the answer that Christianity gives to the people who live this real life. I began to study Christianity and to study that which directs people's lives within the Christian teaching. I began to study the Christianity that I saw applied in daily life and began to compare that applied belief with its source. The source of the Christian teaching was the Gospels, and in these Gospels I came upon an explanation for that meaning that directed the lives of all the people that I saw living the real life. But studying Christianity, I found next to this source of the pure water of life an illegitimate intermixture of dirt and muck that had obscured its purity for me; mingled with the high Christian teaching I found foreign and ugly teachings from church and Hebrew tradition. I was in the position of a man who has received a stinking sack of filth and after much labor and struggle finds that in this sack full of filth, priceless pearls actually lie hidden, a man who realizes that he is not to blame for his feeling of repulsion from the stinking filth and that not only are the people who gathered and preserved these pearls in the dirt not to be blamed, that they are in fact worthy of respect, but a man who nevertheless does not know what he ought to do with those precious things he has found mixed in with the filth. I found myself in this tormented position until I became convinced that the pearls had not fused with the filth and could be cleaned.

I did not know the light and I thought there was no truth in life. But having become convinced that people could only live by this light, I began to seek its source and I found it in the Gospels, despite the false interpretations of the churches. And having arrived at this source of light, I was blinded by it and was given full answers to my questions concerning the meaning of my life and the lives of others, answers that completely harmonized with all the answers from the other cultures familiar to me, answers that, in my opinion, transcended all others.

I sought the answer to the question of life, not to theological or historical questions. Therefore it was completely irrelevant to me whether or not Jesus Christ was God and where the Holy Ghost comes from and so on, and it was equally unimportant and unnecessary to know when and by whom which Gospel and which parable was written and whether or not it could be ascribed to Jesus. To me, what was important was the light which had illuminated eighteen hundred years of humanity and which had illuminated and still illuminates me. However, what to call that light, what its materials are, and who lit it was entirely irrelevant to me.

I began to look deeply into that light and toss away all that was opposed to it, and the further I went along this path, the more undoubtable the difference between truth and falsehood became for me. At the beginning of my work, I still had doubts and there were attempts at artificial explanations, but the further I went, the firmer and clearer the task became and the more irrefutable the truth. I was in the position of a man gathering together the pieces of a broken statue. At the beginning there may still have been uncertainty as to whether a given piece was part of the leg or the arm, but once the legs had been fully reassembled, it became clear that a certain piece probably was not part of the leg and when, moreover, the piece seemed to fit with some other part of the torso and all the fracture lines seemed to align properly with the other pieces, then there could no longer be any doubt. I experienced this as I made forward progress in my work, and unless I am insane, then the reader should also experience that feeling when reading the larger account of the Gospel, where every thesis is confirmed directly by philological considerations, variants, contexts and concordance with the fundamental idea.

We might end the foreword on that point, if only the Gospels were newly revealed books, if the teaching of Christ hadn't undergone eighteen hundred years of false interpretations. But now, in order to understand the true teaching of Christ, as he might have understood it himself, it is important to realize the main reason for these false interpretations that have spoiled the teaching and the main approaches these false interpretations take. The main reason for these false interpretations that have so disfigured the teaching of Christ, to such a degree that it is hard to even see it beneath the layer of fat, is the fact that since the time of Paul, who did not understand Christ's teachings very well and did not hear it as it would later be expressed in the Gospel of Matthew, Christ's teachings have been connected with the pharisaical tradition and by extension all the teachings of the Old Testament. Paul is usually considered the apostle of the gentiles—the apostle of the Protestants. He was that on the surface, in his relationship to circumcision, for example. But the teaching about tradition, about the connection of the Old Testament with the New, was introduced into Christianity by Paul. This very teaching on tradition, this principle of tradition, was the main reason that the Christian teaching was distorted and misread.

The Christian Talmud begins at the time of Paul, calling itself the church, and thus the teaching of Christ ceases to be unified, divine and self-contained, but becomes just one of the links in a chain of revelations which began at the start of the world and which continues in the church up to this time.

These false readings refer to Jesus as God. However, professing him to be a God does not prompt them to attribute the words and teaching of this supposed God any more significance than the words they find in the Pentateuch, the Psalms, the Acts of the apostles, the Epistles, Revelation or even the collected decrees and writings of the fathers of the church.

These false interpretations allow no other understanding of the teaching of Jesus Christ than what would be in agreement with all preceding and subsequent revelation. So their goal is not to genuinely explain the sense of Christ's sermons, but only to find the least contradictory meaning for all the most hopelessly conflicting writings: the Pentateuch, the Psalms, the Gospels, the Epistles, the Acts, i.e., in everything that is considered scripture.

With such an approach to Christ's teaching, it is obvious that it would become incomprehensible. All of the innumerable disagreements on how to understand the Gospel flow out of this false approach. One might guess—and guess correctly—that these explanations, which are interested primarily in reconciling the ir-reconcilable, i.e., the Old and New Testaments, would be innumer-able. So, in order to profess this reconciliation as truth we must have recourse to external means: miracles and the visitation of the Holy Ghost.

Everyone reconciled the differences in their own way, and such reconciling continues today; but in their reconciliation, everyone asserts that their words are the continued revelation of the Holy Ghost. Paul's epistles follow this model, as does the founding of the church councils, which begin with the formula: "It pleases us and the Holy Ghost." Such too are the decrees of the popes, synods, khlysts* and all false interpreters who claim that the Holy Ghost speaks through their mouths. They all rely on the same crude plat-form to confirm the truth of their reconciliation, they all claim that their reconciliation is not the fruit of their own thoughts, but the testimony of the Holy Ghost.

When one refuses to enter this fray of faiths, each of which calls itself true, it becomes impossible not to notice that in their common approach, wherein they accept the enormous amount of so-called scripture in the Old and New Testaments to be uniformly sacred, there lies an insurmountable self-constructed obstacle to under-standing the teaching of Christ. Moreover, one notices that it is from this delusion that the opportunity and even necessity for end-lessly varied and hostile sects arises.

Only the reconciling of an enormous amount of revelations can foster endless variety. Interpreting the teaching of one indi-vidual, who is worshipped as a God, cannot give birth to a sect.

* A splinter sect of ascetics, in existence from the seventeenth to twentieth centuries, that broke off from the Russian Orthodox Church.

The teaching of a God who has descended to earth in order to instruct people cannot be interpreted in different ways because this would be counter to the very goal of descending. If God descended to earth in order to reveal truth to people, then the very least he could have done would be to have revealed the truth in such a way that everybody would understand it. If he did not do this, then he was not God. If God's truths are such that even God couldn't make them understandable to people, then of course there's no way that people could have done it.

If Jesus isn't God, but was a great man, then his teachings are even less likely to give birth to sects. The teachings of a great man can only be considered great if he clearly and understandably expresses that which others have only expressed unclearly and incomprehensibly.

That which is incomprehensible in the teaching of a great man is simply not great and the teaching of a great man cannot give birth to a sect. The teaching of a great man is only great insofar as it unifies people in a single truth for all. The teaching of Socrates has always been understood uniformly by all. Only the kind of interpretation which claims to be the revelation of the Holy Ghost, to be the only truth, and that all else is a lie, only this kind of interpretation can give birth to hatred and the so-called sects. No matter how much the members of a given denomination speak of how they do not judge other denominations, how they pray for communion with them and have no hatred toward them, it is not so. Never, going back to Arius, has any claim, regardless of its supporting dogma, arisen from anything other than condemnation of the falseness of the opposing dogma. To contend that the expression of a given dogma is a divine expression, that it is of the Holy Ghost, is the highest degree of pride and stupidity: the highest pride because it is impossible to say anything more prideful than, "The words that I speak are said through me by God himself," and the highest stupidity because when responding to another man's claim that God speaks through his mouth, it is impossible to say anything more stupid than, "No, it is not through your mouth that God speaks, he speaks through my mouth and he says the complete opposite of what your God is saying." But, all along, this is exactly what every church claims, and it is from this very thing that all the sects have arisen as well as all the evil in the world that has been done and is being done in the name of faith. But apart from the outward evil that is produced by the sects' interpretations, there is another important, internal deficiency that gives all of these sects an unclear, murky and dishonest character.

With all the sects, this deficiency can be detected in the fact that, although they acknowledge the last revelation of the Holy Ghost to be its descent onto the apostles and subsequent passage down to the supposedly chosen ones, these false interpreters never express directly, concretely, and definitively what exactly that revelation from the Holy Ghost is. Yet all the while it is upon this supposed continued revelation that they base their faith and by which they consider this faith to be Christ's.

All the leaders of the churches who claim the revelation of the Holy Ghost recognize, as do the Muslims, three revelations. The Muslims recognize Moses, Jesus and Mohammed. The church leaders recognize Moses, Jesus and the Holy Ghost. But according to the Muslim faith, Mohammed was the last prophet, the one who explained the meaning of Moses's and Jesus's revelations; he is the last revelation, explaining all that came before, and every true believer holds to this revelation. But it is not so with the church belief. It recognizes, like the Muslim faith, three revelations—Moses's, Jesus's and the Holy Ghost's—but it does not call itself by the name of the final revelation. Instead, it asserts that the foundation of its faith is the teaching of Christ. Therefore the teachings they propagate are their own, but they ascribe their authority to Christ.

Some sectarians of the Holy Ghost variety consider the final revelation, the one that explained all that preceded it, to be that of Paul, some consider it to be that of certain councils, some that of others, some that of the popes, some that of the patriarchs, some that of private revelations from the Holy Ghost. All of them ought to have named their faith after the one who received that final revelation. If that final revelation is from the church fathers, or the epistles of the Eastern patriarchs, or papal edicts, or the Syllabus of Errors, or the catechism of Luther or Filaret, then say so. Name your faith after that, because the final revelation which explains all previous revelation will always be the most important revelation. However, they do not do this; instead they promote teachings completely foreign to Christ, and claim that Christ himself preached these things. Therefore, according to their teachings, it turns out that Christ announced that he was saving the human race, fallen since Adam, with his own blood, that God is a trinity, that the Holy Ghost descended upon the apostles and spread via the laying on of hands onto the priesthood, that seven sacraments are needed for salvation, that communion ought to occur in two forms, and so on. It turns out that all of this is the teaching of Christ, whereas in Jesus's actual teaching there isn't the slightest hint of any of this. These false teachers should call their teaching and their faith the teaching and faith of the Holy Ghost, not of Christ. The faith of Christ can only rightfully refer to a faith based on Christ's revelation as it comes down to us in the Gospels, and which recognizes this as the ultimate revelation. This is in accordance with Christ's own words: "Do not recognize any as your teacher, except Christ." This concept seems so simple that it should not even be a point of discussion, but strange as it may be to say so, to this day, nobody has attempted to separate the teaching of Christ from that artificial and completely unjustified reconciliation with the Old Testament or from those arbitrary additions to his teachings that were made

and are still being made in the name of the Holy Ghost. What is
even stranger to see in this error is the convergence of two camps
on the extreme edges of the debate: the church leaders and the free-
thinking historians of Christianity. One group, the church leaders, calling Jesus the second personage of the trinity, understand
his teaching only through the filter of the supposed revelations of
the third personage, whom they find in the Old Testament, in the
epistles of the councils and the edicts of the church fathers. As a
result, they preach the most peculiar principles, claiming that these
principles are Christ's. In just the same way, the other group, not
recognizing Christ as a God, does not understand his teaching as
he might actually have expressed it, but as Paul and the other interpreters have understood it. Considering Christ to be a man and
not a God, these interpreters deprive Christ of the most legitimate
human right to answer for one's own words and not for another's
false reading of them. In trying to explain the teaching of Jesus,
these scholarly interpreters entwine Jesus in ideas he never would
have thought to speak. The representatives of this school of interpreters, beginning with the most popular of them, Renan, make
no attempt to separate from Christ's teaching—from what Christ
himself actually taught—all that has been calcified onto it by his
interpreters, and so, they make no more effort to understand this
teaching than do the church leaders. They attempt to understand
Christ as a phenomenon and to understand the proliferation of Jesus's teaching through the events of his life and the conditions of
his time.

It goes without saying that these historians should not allow
themselves to be making this mistake. The problem that stands
before them to solve is the following: eighteen hundred years ago,
some sort of poor person showed up and said something. He was
cut down and hung up and everyone forgot about him, just as mil-
lions of such instances have been forgotten, and for two hundred

years the world did not hear a thing about him. But then, it turns out, somebody remembered him and what he had said and so he told it to another person and then to a third. And so on and so on, to the point that billions of people, smart and stupid, learned and illiterate, cling to the thought that this man, and only this man, was God. How can we explain this amazing phenomenon? The church leaders say that this occurred because Jesus actually was God. So everything makes sense. But if he was not God, then how can we explain that this man, specifically, is recognized by all as God?

And the scholars of this school earnestly attempt to uncover all the details of the conditions of this man's life, paying no attention to the fact that no matter how much they seek out these details (and all they do is refer to what was printed in Josephus Flavius and the Gospels, they don't actually seek anything out), even if they were to completely reconstruct Jesus's life to the most minute details and discover when he ate a certain thing or where he slept, the question of why he—specifically he—had such an influence on people would remain, all the same, unanswered. The answer is not to be found in the environment where Jesus was born, who it was that raised him and so on, and it is even less to be found in what was taking place in Rome at the time and whether the people tended toward superstition and so on, but only in what this man preached, what was so special that it forced people to place him apart from all the others and recognize him as a God both then and now. It would seem that if you really want to understand this, then the first thing you would need to do is attempt to understand the teaching of this man and, it goes without saying, understand his actual teaching and not the vulgar interpretations of that teaching that were spread and are still being spread after him. But they do not do this. These scholarly historians of Christianity are so overjoyed with their understanding that Jesus was not a God and they want so badly to prove that his teaching was not divine and that it is therefore unnecessary. They forget that the more they try to prove that he was just a simple man and that his teaching was not divine, the further they will be from answering the question they are trying to solve, because they are wasting all their energy proving him a simple man and his teaching not divine. To see this delusion clearly, it would be worth looking at Renan and his followers: Havet, who naively asserts that Jesus Christ *n'avait rien de chritien*, and Souris, who demonstrates with great joy that Jesus was an exceptionally rude and stupid man.

The task is not to prove that Jesus was not a God and that therefore his teachings were not divine, any more than it is to prove that he was Catholic. The task must be to understand the essence of his teaching, this teaching that became so high and precious for people that they recognized the messenger of it as a God. I have tried to do this very thing; for myself at least, I have done it. And now I am offering it to my brothers.

If the reader belongs to the enormous majority of the educated, raised in the church faith, who have not strayed from that faith despite its incongruity with good common sense and conscience (for such a man, love and respect for the spirit of the Christian teaching must remain, otherwise, as in the proverb, he "throws the fur coat onto the fire because he is angry at the fleas," considering all of Christianity a dangerous superstition), then I ask such a reader to consider that what pushes him away and what he deems superstition is not the teaching of Christ and that Christ can in no way be blamed for the repulsive beliefs that have been stitched onto his teaching and presented as Christianity. One must study the teaching of Christ alone, insofar as we have access to it—that is, those words and actions which have been attributed to Christ and which have an instructive meaning. Reading my account, such a reader will be convinced that Christianity not only is not a mixture of high and low, not only is it not superstitious, but that, on the contrary, it is the strictest, purest and fullest metaphysical and ethical teaching, above which no other human intellect has ascended to this day and in the radiance of which, though it may not do so consciously, all higher human activity operates: political, scientific, poetic and philosophical. If the reader belongs to that insignificant minority of educated people who cling to church faith, confessing it not for any external purposes but for inner peace, then I ask such a reader, before reading, to decide first in his soul, which is more valuable to him: spiritual peace or truth? If it is peace, then I ask him not to read; if it is truth, then I ask him to remember that the teaching of Christ, laid out here, despite the identical name, is a completely different teaching than the one he confesses, and that therefore the relationship of someone who confesses church faith to this account of Christ's teaching is the same as the relationship of the Muslims to the sermons of Christianity. The question for him is not does this teaching in question agree with his faith or not, but only which teaching agrees more with his mind and heart. Is it the church teaching, which is founded on a reconciliation of all the scriptures, or is it the teaching of Christ on its own. For him, the question can only be framed like this: Does he want to accept a new teaching or remain in his own faith?

If the reader belongs to the group of people who externally claim church faith and value it not because they believe in its truth but because of external considerations, since they consider its ritual and preaching appropriate to their lifestyle, then let such people remember that no matter how many kindred thinkers they may have, no matter how strong they may be, no matter which thrones they may sit on, whichever high names they may call themselves, they are not in the position of the accusers, but of the accused, and not by me, but by Christ. Let such readers remember that they said what they had to say a long time ago and that even if they proved what they want to prove, they would merely be proving what all the hundreds of contradictory church faiths prove for themselves. They should remember that they have no need to prove anything; they should instead justify themselves. Justify themselves in the sacrilege of equating the teaching of Jesus the God with that of Ezdra, that of the councils and that of Theophylact and the sacrilege of allowing themselves to overinterpret the word of God and alter it based on the words of people. Justify themselves in slandering God, which they did by taking all the fanaticism that was in their hearts and dumping it on Jesus the God and passing it off as his teaching. Justify themselves in the fraud of hiding the teaching of God that was sent to bring goodness into the world, and putting in its place their own Holy Ghost faith. With this replacement they have deprived and continue to deprive billions of people of the goodness which Christ brought to the people, and in place of the peace and love he brought, they have brought sects into the world, along with judgments and all manner of evil, twisting it all in the name of Christ.

For those readers there are only two alternatives: humble repentance and renunciation of these lies or persecution of those who can expose them for what they have done and are still doing.

If they do not renounce their lies, they have only one choice: to persecute me. And having finished my writing, I now prepare for this with joy and with fear for my weakness.

—*Leo Tolstoy*

The Gospel

*A Proclamation on Goodness from Jesus
Christ, the Son of God*

KNOWLEDGE OF LIFE

Jesus Christ's proclamation replaced faith in an external God with a knowledge of life.

The Gospel proclaims that the source of all things is not an external God, as people think, but a knowledge of life. And therefore, in place of that which people call God, the Gospel posits a knowledge of life.

Without knowledge there is no life. Every man is living only because he has knowledge. Those people who do not understand this and propose the flesh as the source of life deprive themselves of true life. But those who understand that they live not by the flesh but by knowledge are the ones who have true life. And Jesus Christ demonstrated this true life. Realizing the truth that man's life comes from knowledge, he gave people a teaching and a model life of knowledge in the flesh.

Previous doctrines expressed themselves as laws dictating what one must do and not do in order to serve God. The teaching of Jesus Christ is based on a knowledge of life. No one has seen and no one can know the external God, and therefore the service of an external God cannot govern life. The path of life can only be seen when one recognizes that the knowledge located within, as it arises from the source of all knowledge, is the basis for everything.*

---

* At the beginning of each chapter, Tolstoy composed a summary of the verses contained in the given chapter. In distilling the Gospel teachings even further, these summaries sometimes take a slightly different approach to the content, one in which the author's opinion is more apparent. These summaries are presented here in italics.

In the beginning stood the knowledge of life, as the foundation of all things. Knowledge of life stood in the place of God. Knowledge of life is God. According to Jesus's proclamation, it stands as the basis and source of all things, in the place of God.

All that lives was born into life through knowledge. And without it, there can be nothing living.

Knowledge gives true life.

Knowledge is the light of life. It is the light that shines in the darkness and the darkness cannot extinguish it. The true light has always been in the world and it illuminates every person born into the world. It was in the world and the world is living only because it had that light of knowledge within itself, but the world did not hold on to it.

It revealed itself to its own, but its own did not keep it. Only the ones who understood the knowledge, they alone were given the opportunity to become like it, by virtue of their belief in its essence. Those who believed in the fact that life is based in knowledge did not become sons of the flesh, but became sons of knowledge.

And the knowledge of life manifested itself in the flesh, through the person of Jesus Christ, and we understood his meaning—that the son of knowledge, a man in the flesh, the only begotten of the father, begotten from the source of life, is the same as the father, the same as the source of life.

The teaching of Jesus is the perfect and true faith. Because by fulfilling the teaching of Jesus we have come to understand a new faith in place of the old. The law had been given through Moses, but we have come to understand the true faith, based on the attaining of knowledge, through Jesus Christ.

Nobody has seen God and nobody ever will; only the son, the one who is within the father, he alone has shown the path of life.

Chapter One

THE SON OF GOD

Man, the son of God, is powerless in the flesh
and free in the spirit.

OUR FATHER

Jesus was the son of an unknown father. Not knowing his own father, he referred to God as his father during his childhood. In Judea at that time there was a prophet named John, who prophesied the coming of God to earth. He said that if people would change their lives, consider all people equal among themselves, not harm each other but instead help one another, then God would come down to earth and his kingdom would be established on earth. Hearing this sermon, Jesus leaves the company of people and goes into the desert in order to understand the meaning of the life of man and his relationship to the endless source of all things, that which is called God.

After a few days in the wilderness without food, Jesus begins to wither from hunger, and he thinks, "I am the son of the almighty God and therefore should be as almighty as he is; but here I am, hungry, and bread does not appear according to my will. So it would seem that I am not almighty." After this, he says to himself, "I cannot turn these rocks into bread, but I can abstain from eating bread. And therefore, if I am not almighty in the flesh, I am almighty in spirit—I can conquer the flesh. Therefore I am the son of God, not in the flesh but in spirit."

"But if I am the son in spirit," he says to himself further, "I can renounce the flesh and destroy it." And to that he answers, "I was born by

[5]

the spirit in the flesh. Such was the will of my father, and therefore I cannot oppose his will."

"But, if you cannot satisfy your desires in the flesh and cannot renounce the flesh," he says to himself further, "then you should work for the flesh and savor all of the pleasures that it gives you." And to that he answers, "I cannot satisfy the desires of the flesh and cannot renounce the flesh, but my life becomes almighty within the spirit of my father and therefore in the flesh I should serve and work for the one spirit alone—the spirit of the father."

And convincing himself that the life of man can only be within the father, Jesus leaves the wilderness and begins to preach to the people. He says that the spirit is within him, that from now on heaven is wide open and that the heavenly powers are united with man, that free and endless life has begun for people, and that all people, no matter how unlucky they might be in the flesh, may be blessed.

————————

The birth of Jesus Christ happened like this: His mother, Mary, was engaged to Joseph. But before they began to live as husband and wife, it happened that Mary became pregnant. This Joseph was a good man and did not want to disgrace Mary; he took her as his wife and had no relations with her until she gave birth to her first son and named him Jesus.

And the boy grew up and became a young man. And he was intelligent beyond his years.

Jesus was already twelve years old when, once, Mary and Joseph went to Jerusalem for a holiday and took the boy with them. The holiday passed and they departed for home, having forgotten the boy. Then they remembered him and thought that he must have run off with the other boys, so they asked about him along the road.

The boy was nowhere to be found and so they returned to Jerusalem after him.

And after three days they found him in a church, where he sat with the teachers, asking them things and listening. And everyone was amazed at his intelligence.

His mother saw him and said, "What have you done to us? Your father and I are full of grief, searching for you."

And he said to them, "Where did you look for me? Don't you know that you should look for the son in the house of his father?"

And they did not understand his words; they did not understand who it was that he called his father. After that Jesus lived with his mother and obeyed her in everything. And he developed in both age and knowledge. And everyone thought that Jesus was the son of Joseph.

And so he lived until he was thirty years old.

At that time the prophet John made himself known in Judea. John lived in the Judean steppes, on the Jordan. John's clothing was made of camel hair and was tied with a belt, and he subsisted on tree bark and wild plants.

He challenged the people to change their lives in order to free themselves of error, and as a sign of this life change, he bathed the people in the river Jordan.

He said, "A voice is calling to you; pave God's path in the wilderness, make the path that leads to him level. Make all things even, let there be no dips and no rises, nothing high and nothing low. Then God will be within you and everyone will find their own salvation."

And the people asked him, "What should we do?"

He answered, "Whoever has two articles of clothing, give them to him who has none. And whoever has food, give it to him who has none."

THE GOSPEL IN BRIEF

And the tax collectors came to him and asked, "What should we do?"

He said to them, "Do not collect more than you are required to."

And the soldiers asked, "How should we behave?"

He said, "Do not offend anyone, do not cheat. Be content with what you have been granted."

And the citizens of Jerusalem came to him, as did all the Jews in the vicinity of Jordan. And they repented to him for their evil actions, and as a sign of their change of life, he bathed them in the Jordan.

And the orthodox and old believers also came to John, but secretly.

He detected their presence and said, "You snakelike breed, apparently you have already sensed that it is impossible to withstand God's will. So then, alter your thinking and change your faith. And if you want to change your faith, then let it be visible by your fruits that you have altered your thinking.

"The axe has already been placed near the tree. If the tree produces bad fruit, it is cut down and thrown into the fire. As a sign of the change in your faith, I purify you with water, but after this bathing you must still be purified with the spirit. The spirit will purify you like the master purifies his threshing floor: he gathers the wheat and burns the chaff."

Jesus came from Galilee to Jordan in order to be bathed by John, and he was bathed and listened to John's sermon.

And from Jordan he went into the desert, where he came to know the power of the spirit. Jesus spent forty days and forty nights in the desert with no drink and no food.

And the voice of the flesh said to him, "If you were the son of the almighty God, then you could, of your own will, make bread from these rocks, but you cannot do that, so it would seem that you are not the son of God."

But Jesus said to himself, "If I cannot turn rocks into bread, then that means that I am not the son of the God of the flesh, but the son of the God of the spirit. I live not on bread, but on spirit. And my spirit can disregard the flesh." But all the same, hunger tormented him and the voice of the flesh spoke to him more, "If you live on spirit and can disregard the flesh, then you can renounce the flesh and your spirit will remain living."

And he imagined that he stood on the roof of the temple and the voice of the flesh said to him, "If you are the son of God, then when you throw yourself from the temple, you will not be killed. But an unseen power will preserve you, support you and deliver you from any evil."

But Jesus said to himself, "I can disregard the flesh, but I cannot renounce it entirely, because I was born into the flesh by the spirit. Such was the will of the father of my spirit and I cannot oppose him."

Then the voice of the flesh said to him, "If you cannot oppose your father in the matter of throwing yourself off the temple and renouncing the flesh, then you also cannot oppose your father in the matter of going hungry when you want to eat. You should not disregard the lusts of the flesh. They have been placed in you and you should serve them."

And all the kingdoms of the earth and all of its people were presented to Jesus, how they live and labor for the flesh, expecting from it some reward.

And the voice of the flesh said to him, "There, you see, they work for me and I give them everything that they want. If you work for me, you will get that as well."

But Jesus said to himself, "My father is not flesh, but spirit. I live by it, I sense it in myself at all times. I respect it alone and work for it alone, and I expect rewards from it alone."

Then the temptation ceased and Jesus came to know the power of the spirit.

Having come to know the power of the spirit, Jesus left the desert and came to John again and stayed with him. And when the time came for Jesus to leave John, John said of him, "That is a savior of people."

At these words from John, two of John's students left their former teacher and followed after Jesus.

Jesus saw that they were following him, stopped, and said to them, "What do you need?"

They said to him, "Teacher! We want to be with you and learn your teaching."

He said, "Then come with me and I will tell you everything."

They set off with him and remained with him, listening to him until the tenth hour.

One of these students was called Andrew. Andrew had a brother, Simon. Having listened to Jesus, Andrew went to his brother Simon and said to him, "We have found the one that the prophets and Moses wrote about, the one who will proclaim our salvation to us."

Andrew took Simon with him and brought him along to Jesus. Jesus named this brother of Andrew's Peter, which means "rock." And both of these brothers became students of Jesus.

Then, just as they entered into Galilee, Jesus met Philip and called for him to come along. Philip was from Beth-saida, the same village as Peter and Andrew.

When Philip recognized Jesus, he went and sought out his brother Nathaniel and said to him, "We have found God's chosen one, about whom the prophets and Moses wrote. It is Jesus, the son of Joseph, from Nazareth."

Nathaniel was amazed by this, that the one the prophets had written about was from the neighboring village, and he said, "Strange that this messenger of God is from Nazareth."

Philip said, "Come with me, you will see and hear for yourself."

Nathaniel agreed and went with his brother and met with Jesus. And when he had heard him out, he said to Jesus, "Yes, now I see that it is true, that you are the son of God and the King of Israel."

Jesus said to him, "You must learn what is even more important than that. From now on you will learn that heaven is open and that people can communicate with the powers of heaven. From now on, God will no longer be separated from his people."

And Jesus returned to the place of his birth in Nazareth. And on the holy day he went, as always, to the meeting and began to read. He was given the book of Isaiah. He opened it and read what was written in the book: "The spirit of the Lord is within me. He chose me to proclaim goodness to the unhappy and the brokenhearted, to proclaim freedom to the bound, light to the blind and salvation and rest to the exhausted. To announce to all that this is the time of God's mercy."

He closed the book, gave it to the attendant, and sat down; and everyone waited to hear what he would say.

And he said, "Now this verse has been fulfilled before your eyes."

Chapter Two

GOD IS A SPIRIT

And therefore man should work, not for the flesh,
but for the spirit.

WHO ART IN HEAVEN

Considering themselves to be orthodox believers, the Jews revere the external God, the creator of the flesh. According to their teaching, this external God had made an agreement with them, wherein he promised to help the Jews, and the Jews had promised to reverence him, and the main condition of this agreement was the observance of the Sabbath. Jesus rejected the observance of the Sabbath. He says, "The Sabbath is an institution of man. A living man is more important in his spirit than all external rituals. Observance of the Sabbath ritual, like all external worship, contains a fallacy at its core. It is impossible to do nothing on the Sabbath. A man should do good deeds at all times, and if the Sabbath is preventing the doing of a good deed, then that means the Sabbath is a lie."

The orthodox Jews considered another condition of this agreement to be the avoidance of interaction with non-believers. To this, Jesus says that God does not want sacrifices from people, but love between them.

They considered one more condition of the agreement to be the rules of ablution and purification. Addressing this, Jesus states that God does not demand external purity but demands only charity and love toward other people.

Jesus makes the point that external ordinances are harmful and that church traditions themselves are evil. Church traditions make it so that people throw out the most important acts of love—for example, love for one's father and mother—and justify it with church tradition.

Concerning all things external, all the rules of the previous law that determined those situations in which a person might become defiled, Jesus says, "You all know that nothing can defile a person from the outside; only what he thinks can defile a person."

Jesus comes to Jerusalem, a city considered to be holy, and he goes into the temple, where the orthodox believed God himself lived, and he says that it is unnecessary to make sacrifices to God, that a person is more important than the temple, and that all one must do is love and help his neighbor.

One need not worship God in some special place, instead one must serve God in deed and in spirit. The spirit is impossible to see or to show. The spirit is a person's consciousness of their status as a son of the endless spirit. A temple is not necessary. The true temple is the world of people, united in love. All external worship is not only false and harmful when it facilitates evil deeds, but it is harmful because the person that fulfills external ordinances considers himself correct and frees himself from the need to perform any acts of love. The only person who strives for goodness and performs acts of love is the one who feels his own imperfection. External worship leads to the error of self-satisfaction, therefore all external worship is unnecessary and should be thrown out. It is impossible to combine acts of love with the fulfillment of ordinances and impossible under the guise of external worship to perform acts of love. Man is the son of God in spirit, and therefore he should serve the father in spirit.

It happened that once, on the Sabbath, Jesus was walking through a field with his students. The students had gotten hungry and along the way had torn off some heads of grain, plucked the kernels with their hands and began to eat. But according to the orthodox teaching, God had established a covenant with Moses that required all to observe the Sabbath and to do nothing at all on the Sabbath day. According to the orthodox teaching, God had commanded that whoever worked on the Sabbath should be beaten with stones.

The orthodox saw that the students were plucking the ears of corn on the Sabbath and they said, "That is not to be done on the Sabbath. We are forbidden to work on the Sabbath and yet you are plucking ears of corn. God established the Sabbath and commanded that its violation be punished by death."

Jesus heard this and said, "If you understood what these words of God mean, 'I want love and not sacrifice,' you would not be condemning them for something which bears no guilt. Man is more important than the Sabbath."

It happened on another Sabbath as Jesus was teaching in a meeting that a sick woman approached him and asked him to help her. And Jesus began to care for her.

Then, an orthodox church elder became angry at Jesus for this and said to the people, "In God's law it is said 'There are six days in the week for work.'"

And at this, Jesus asked the orthodox legalists, "What, then, in your opinion, is it also forbidden to help another person on the Sabbath?"

And they did not know what to answer.

Then Jesus said, "Deceivers! Don't each of you untether your animal from the manger and lead it to drink on the Sabbath? And if someone's sheep falls into the well, then of course, does he not run and pull it out, even if it is the Sabbath?"

Once, Jesus saw a tax collector gathering taxes. This tax collector was named Matthew. Jesus spoke with him and Matthew understood him, came to love his teaching, and called him to his home as a guest, preparing refreshments for him.

When Jesus came to Matthew, some acquaintances, tax collectors and non-believers, were visiting him. But Jesus did not shun them and sat down himself, as did his students.

And now the orthodox saw this and said to Jesus's students, "How is it that your teacher is eating with tax collectors and these other wayward people? On the contrary, according to orthodox law, God has commanded us not to communicate with the non-believing."

Jesus heard this and said, "Whoever rejoices in his health has no need for a healer, but whoever is sick needs one. Understand what God's words mean: 'I want love, not sacrifice.' It is impossible for me to teach those who consider themselves orthodox to change their faith, so instead I teach those who consider themselves wayward."

The orthodox legalists came to Jesus from Jerusalem. And they saw that his students and he himself ate bread with unwashed hands. And the orthodox legalists began to condemn him for this, because they themselves behaved strictly according to church tradition, such as their requirement for washing dishes: if they are not washed properly, they do not eat off of them. And also, after making their purchases, they will not eat anything if they do not wash it first.

And the orthodox legalists asked him, "What is your reason for not living by church tradition but taking your bread and eating it with unwashed hands?"

And he answered them, "How is it that you break the commandments of God by living the church traditions? God has told you: honor your father and mother. And you came up with the idea that everyone can say: I offer to God what I would have given to my parents. And then you can go without feeding your father and mother.

That is how you break the commandments of God with church tradition.

"Deceivers! The prophet Isaiah spoke the truth of you: 'Because this people only prostrates itself before me in words and honors me with its tongue, while its heart is far from me, and because its fear before me is only a requirement of man, which it has memorized, for that I will perform an amazing and peculiar act for this people: the wisdom of its wise men will tumble and the intelligence of its educated ones will fade. Woe to those who trouble themselves to hide their desires from the Eternal and who perform their acts in the dark.'

"Just so, you leave behind what is important in the law, the portion that is God's commandment, and you live your own human traditions, cleaning off cups."

And Jesus called together all the people and said, "Listen all of you, and understand. There is nothing in the world that can enter into a person and defile him, but what comes out of him, that is what defiles a person. Let there be love and charity in your soul and then everything will be clean. Try to understand this."

And when he returned home, his students asked him what those words meant.

And he said, "Even you did not understand? Don't you understand that all things external and mortal cannot defile a person? Because it enters his belly and not his soul. It enters his belly and exits out of his rear with the excrement. Only what comes out of a person, what comes out of his soul, can defile a person.

"This is because evil comes from a person's soul: fornication, bawdiness, murder, thievery, greed, malice, deceit, insolence, jealousy, slander, pride and all kinds of foolishness. All of this evil comes from a person's soul and only these things can defile a person."

After this, Passover approached and Jesus came to Jerusalem and went into the temple.

At the porch of the temple there stood livestock: cows, bulls, and rams. A cage for doves had been built there as well. Behind this, booths were set up for moneychangers with their money. All of this was necessary in order to make offerings to God. They killed and made the offering in the temple. This was the method of prayer for the Jews, as it had been taught to them by the orthodox legalists.

Jesus entered the temple, brandished a whip, drove out all the livestock from the porch, set free all of the doves and scattered all of the money. And he commanded that none of these things be carried into the temple.

He said, "The prophet Isaiah said to you, 'The house of God is not the temple in Jerusalem, but the whole world of God's people.' And in addition, the prophet Jeremiah said to you, 'Do not believe false speeches concerning how this is the home of the Eternal. Do not believe that, but instead change your life and do not judge falsely, do not oppress the traveler, the widow or the orphan, do not spill innocent blood and do not come to the house of God and say: Now we can do our obscenities in peace. Do not think that a den of bandits could be the home of the father.' "

And the Jews took up the argument and said to him, "You say that our worship service is incorrect; how are you going to prove this?"

And, turning to address them, Jesus said, "Tear down this temple and in three days I will raise a new, living temple."

And the Jews said, "How will you make a new temple now, when it took forty-six years to build this one?"

And Jesus told them, "I am speaking to you about something that is more important than the temple. You would not be saying these things if you understood what these words of the prophets mean: 'I, God, do not rejoice in your offerings, but I rejoice in your love one to another.' The living temple is the whole world of people when they love one another."

And then in Jerusalem, many people began to believe in what he had said. But he himself did not believe in anything external because he knew that all things are within a person. He did not need anybody to teach him about man, because he knew that inside of a man is a soul.

And once, Jesus had to travel through Samaria. He walked by the village of the Samaritan Sychar, nearby the place that Jacob had given to his son Joseph. Jacob's well was located there. Jesus was weary from the road and sat down at the well, and his students went into the city for bread.

And a woman came out from the Sychar for water. Jesus asked her for something to drink.

And she said to him, "How is it that you are asking me for something to drink? After all, you Jews don't associate with us Samaritans."

And he said to her, "If you knew me and knew what I teach, you would not say this, but would give me something to drink and I would give you the water of life. Whoever drinks his fill of your water will become thirsty again. But whoever drinks his fill of my water will be satisfied forever, and this water of mine will lead him to eternal life."

The woman understood that he was speaking of the divine and said to him, "I see that you are a prophet, if you want to, teach me. But how can you teach me the divine when you are a Jew and I am a Samaritan? Our people pray to God on this mountain and you Jews say that God's house is only in Jerusalem. You cannot teach me the divine because you have one faith and we have another."

And Jesus told her, "Believe me, woman, the time has already arrived when people will cease to pray to the father either here on this mountain or in Jerusalem. Because if they pray to God, then they pray to that which they do not know, but if they pray to the father, then they pray to someone who is impossible not to know.

"The time has come that the real venerators of God will not worship God, but will worship the father in spirit and in action. These are the kind of venerators that the father needs. God is a spirit, and we must worship him in spirit and in action."

The woman could not make out what he had said to her so she said, "I heard that God's messenger was coming, he who is called the anointed one. He will then tell us everything."

And Jesus said to her, "I am that very one, speaking with you now. Do not wait for anyone else."

After that, Jesus came to the land of Judea and lived there with his students and taught. At that time, John taught the people near Salim and bathed them in the river Aenon. Because John still had not been put in prison.

And a debate started up between John's students and Jesus's students about which is better: John's cleansing in water or Jesus's teachings.

And they came to John and said to him, "Now, you purify with water and Jesus only teaches; yet everyone goes to him. What do you say about him?"

John said, "A man cannot teach anything, if God does not teach him. Whoever speaks about earthly things is earthly but if someone speaks of God, then he is from God. It is impossible to prove whether the words they are speaking are from God or not from God. God is a spirit, he is impossible to measure and impossible to prove. Whoever understands the words of the spirit will be able to prove with this understanding that he is from the spirit.

"The father, loving the son, gave everything to him. Whoever believes in the son has eternal life; and whoever does not believe in the son does not have life. God is the spirit within man."

After that, one orthodox believer came to Jesus and invited him into his home for breakfast. He went in and sat at the table. The orthodox believer noticed that he did not wash before breakfast and was amazed.

And Jesus said to him, "You orthodox wash everything on the outside: but are you clean on the inside? Be charitable toward people and all will be clean."

And as he was sitting in the home of the orthodox believer, a woman who had been unfaithful arrived from the city. She had discovered that Jesus was in the home of the orthodox believer and so she went there and brought a flask with perfumes. She knelt at his feet, began to cry and shed tears on his feet, wiped them with her hair and poured perfume from the flask.

The orthodox believer saw this and thought to himself, "He cannot really be a prophet. If he were really a prophet, he would realize what kind of woman this is washing his feet, he would realize that this is an unfaithful woman and he would not allow her to come close enough to touch him."

Jesus guessed at this, turned to him and said, "Should I tell you what I think?"

"Tell me," the man said.

And Jesus said, "Here's what: Two men counted themselves among the debtors of a certain master, one by five hundred pieces of money and the other by fifty pieces. And neither the one nor the other had anything with which to repay the debt. The master pardoned both. So then, according to your thinking, who will love the master more and care for him more?"

And the man said, "Everyone knows that it would be the one who had the larger debt."

Jesus gestured toward the woman and said, "So it is with you and this woman. You consider yourself orthodox and therefore a minor debtor, she considers herself unfaithful and therefore a major debtor. I came to you, into your home, and you did not offer me water for washing my feet; she washes my feet with tears and dries them with her hair. You did not kiss me, but she is kissing my feet. You did not offer me oil to anoint my head, but she is anointing my feet with expensive perfumes.

"He who considers himself orthodox will not perform any acts of love. And he who considers himself unfaithful will perform acts of love. And acts of love will deliver you out of all error."

And he said to her, "Yes, you have delivered yourself from your errors."

Jesus said, "The whole matter with faith is who one considers oneself to be. Whoever considers himself to be good in his faith will not be good; and whoever considers himself to be bad in his faith will be good."

And Jesus said further, "Once two men went into the temple to pray; one was orthodox, the other an unfaithful tax collector. The orthodox believer prayed like this, 'I thank you, Lord, that I am not like others: I am not a miser, not a cheat, not a libertine and not such a scoundrel as this tax collector here. I fast two days a week and I pay a tithe on all my holdings.'

"But the tax collector stood a ways off and didn't dare to look at the heavens, but simply beat himself on the chest and murmured, 'Lord! Look at me, a worthless man.'

"And so? This one was better than the orthodox because he who elevates himself will be lowered and he who lowers himself will be elevated."

And after this, some students of John came to Jesus and said, "Why is it that, along with the orthodox, we fast so much and your students do not fast at all? Because according to the orthodox law, God has commanded us to fast."

And Jesus said to them, "As long as the groom is at the wedding, no one can be sad. It is only when there is no groom that they are sad. If there is life, then there is no need to be sad.

"It is impossible to combine external worship with acts of love. It is impossible to combine the old teaching of external worship with my teaching of performing acts of love toward one's neighbor. To combine my teaching with the old one is the same as tearing a piece of fabric from a new garment and sewing it onto an old one. So you tear apart the new one and fail to repair the old one. One must accept mine in its entirety or the old one in its entirety. And having accepted my teaching, it is impossible to hold on to the old one of purification, fasts, and Sabbaths. Likewise, it is impossible to pour new wine into old skins, because the skins will burst and the new wine will leak out. But new wine must be poured into new skins, and both the one and the other will remain whole."

The following prophecy of Isaiah was fulfilled in Jesus: "The people were in darkness and suddenly they saw the light. People lived in death's gloom and for them, a light suddenly shined out."

And yet another of Isaiah's prophecies came to fruition: "Behold here is my beloved child. My soul delights in him. Because my spirit is within him and he will proclaim truth to all the nations. He does not argue and does not scream and his voice is not to be heard in the streets. In order for the truth to triumph over the lie, he will not tear up the straw and will not blow out the night lights. In his teachings the people will have hope."

And many people followed after him as he walked from city to village proclaiming true goodness.

Chapter Three

THE SOURCE OF KNOWLEDGE

Every person's life sprang from the spirit of the father.

HALLOWED BE THY NAME

Jesus's students ask him to explain the nature of the kingdom of God, which he has been preaching, and he explains, "The kingdom of God that I preach is the same one that John preached. It is based on the fact that all people can be blessed, no matter what their troubles may be in the flesh."

And Jesus says to the people, "John was the first to preach to the people that the kingdom of God is not in the external world but in the souls of people, and because of this he did more than anyone else. He made it so that from this time forward the law and the prophets and all external worship of God should be unnecessary. From his time it has been revealed that every person, depending on their effort, can be in the kingdom, within the will of God the father."

To the question of when the kingdom of God would arrive, Jesus says that the kingdom of God is invisible and that it is not to be found in anything external, but that it is only within people's souls. The beginning and the end of everything is within a person's soul.

To explain the meaning of the kingdom of God, Jesus says that every man, apart from his mortal life and his own conception in the flesh by an earthly father in the womb of an earthly mother, which he understands, will come to know in himself a spirit that is free, intelligent and independent from the flesh. This spirit is eternal, and since it emanates from the Eternal, it is the source of all and is what we refer to as God. We know God only within ourselves. This spirit is the source of our lives and it needs to be placed higher than all else; we must live off of it. When we have made this spirit the basis of life, we receive true, eternal life. That father spirit who planted this spirit in people could not have done so with the goal of deceiving people, intending for people to recognize this eternal spirit in themselves but then to lose it. If this eternal spirit exists inside a person, then it should give eternal life. So therefore, a man who bases his life on this spirit will have eternal life, while the man who does not base his life on this spirit will not have eternal life. People can choose for themselves life and death. Life is in the spirit, death is in the flesh. The life of the spirit is goodness and light; the mortal life of flesh is evil and darkness. To believe in the spirit means to perform acts of goodness; to not believe means to perform acts of evil. Goodness is life, evil is death. Only the spirit gives people life, it is up to the people to either keep it or lose it. Evil does not exist for the spirit. Evil is the imitation of life; it is non-living.

We do not know God, the external creator, the source of all sources. All that we can comprehend of him is that he planted spirit in people and planted, as does a sower, everywhere, not upturning the earth, and the seed that falls on good earth grows, and the one that falls on undesirable ground will die.

After this, the students of John came to ask Jesus whether he was the one about whom John spoke, whether he would reveal the kingdom of God and renew the people in spirit.

Jesus answered and said, "Look and listen, and then tell John whether the kingdom of God has arrived and whether people are being renewed in spirit. Tell him how I preach the kingdom of God.

"In the prophecies, it is said that when the kingdom of God comes, all people will be blessed. Well, then tell him that my kingdom of God is such that the poor are blessed. And that every-one who understands me will be blessed."

And having let John's students go, Jesus began to speak to the people about what sort of kingdom of God it was that John had pro-claimed.

He said, "When you went to be baptized by John in the wilder-ness, what did you go to see? The orthodox legalists also went but did not understand what John was proclaiming. And they considered him worthless. This species, the orthodox legalists, only consider what they invent themselves and hear from each other to be truth and the only law they regard is the one that they invent themselves. But they do not hear and do not comprehend what John said, and what I am saying. From what John said, they only comprehend that he fasted in the wilderness, and so they say, 'He has a devil in him.'

"From what I am saying they have only comprehended that I do not fast and so they say, 'He eats and drinks with tax collectors and sinners, and he is friendly with them.' Like little children on the street, they chatter with one another and are amazed that nobody listens to them. And their wisdom is visible in their actions. If you wanted to see a man dressed up in expensive clothes, well then many people like that are living in the palaces right here.

"What, did you not see this in the wilderness? You think you went there because John was a prophet like the others? Do not think that. John was not a prophet like the others; he was greater than all the prophets. They prophesied what could happen. He pro-claimed to people what is: namely, that the kingdom of God has been and is on the earth. I tell you truly: no one greater than John has ever been born. He announced the kingdom of God on earth and is therefore greater than all.

"The law and the prophets—all of it was necessary to John. And from the time of John until now, it has been proclaimed that the kingdom of God is on the earth and that he who makes the effort will enter it."

And the orthodox came to Jesus and began to ask him how and when the kingdom of God would come.

He answered them, "The kingdom of God that I preach is not the one that previous prophets preached. They said that God would come with various types of visible appearances and I am talking about such a kingdom of God, the coming of which will be impossible to see with the eyes.

"And if they tell you, 'Look, it came or is coming,' or, 'Look, here it is,' do not believe them. The kingdom of God is not in a time or in any place. It is like lightning—it is here, there and everywhere. And it has no time, and no place because the kingdom of God that I preach is within you."

After this, one of the orthodox, from among the leaders of the Jews, Nicodemus, came to Jesus at night and said, "You do not command us to observe the Sabbath, you do not command us to observe the purification law, you do not command us to make sacrifices or to fast; you destroyed the temple, you say of God that he is a spirit and that the kingdom of God is within us. What kind of kingdom of God is that?"

And Jesus answered him, "You must understand that if a person is conceived from heaven, then within him there ought to be something of heaven."

Nicodemus did not understand this and said, "How can a person, if he was conceived from the flesh of a father, then grows old, crawl back into his mother's belly and be conceived again?"

And Jesus answered him, "Understand what I am saying. I am saying that, apart from the flesh, a person is also conceived in the spirit, that therefore each person is conceived in both flesh and spirit and that therefore the kingdom of heaven can exist within him. Flesh comes from flesh. Spirit cannot be born from flesh; only spirit can come from spirit. The spirit is what lives within you, living freely and intelligently and of which you can know no end and no beginning. Every person feels it within themselves. And so, why were you so amazed that I told you that you must be conceived from heaven?"

Nicodemus said, "All the same, I do not believe that it could be so."

Then Jesus said to him, "What kind of teacher are you if you do not understand this! You must understand that I do not base this on any kind of special wisdom; I interpret only that which we all know, and confirm it with what we can all see. How can you believe in what is in heaven if you do not believe in what is on earth, in what is inside yourself?

"No one has ever been to heaven and man is earth's only resident, having come down from heaven, being of heaven himself. Here, we must elevate this heavenly son that exists within man, so that everyone can believe in him and not perish, but have heavenly life instead.

"It was not, after all, to ruin people, but for their benefit that God gave people his son, who is just like him. He offered him, after all, so that everyone would believe in him and not perish but have eternal life instead. It was not, after all, to destroy the people of the world that he delivered his son, life, into the world of people; he delivered his son, life, so that the world would live by means of him. Whoever trusts their life to him will not die, and whoever does not trust their life to him will destroy themselves because they did not trust that there can be life.

"Separation (death) occurs since, when life comes into the world, people themselves move away from it. Life is people's light. Light came into the world, but people prefer darkness to light and do not move toward the light. So whoever does wrong does not move toward the light; therefore his acts are invisible and he deprives himself of life. And whoever lives in truth moves toward the light, therefore his actions are in the light and he has life and unites himself with God.

"The kingdom of God must be understood differently than you have thought, for example, that for all people, at some certain time and in some certain place the kingdom of God will come. Understand it in this way: that in all the world, certain people, those who rely on the heavenly son of mankind, always make themselves sons of the kingdom while the others who do not rely on him are destroyed. The father of that spirit within a person is the father only of those who recognize themselves to be his sons. And therefore, only those that retain within themselves what he gave them can exist in his eyes."

And after that Jesus began to explain to the people what the kingdom of God was and he explained this in parables.

He said, "The spirit father plants the life of knowledge in the world, completely the same as how a farmer sows seeds in his field. He sows over the whole field, not distinguishing where each one may land. And now, some seeds land on the road, and birds fly down and peck at them. And others fall onto the rocks. And they will scarcely grow on the rocks, but will wither because there is nowhere to take root. And still others fall into the brush and the brush chokes the grain, so the stalks rise up, but do not flourish. And others fall onto good earth, those spring up and compensate for the lost seeds and offer up their grain and flourish; some multiplied one hundred times, some sixty and some thirty.

"And just so, God planted the spirit within people, in some it disappears, and in some it returns, multiplied one hundred times. These are the people that make up the kingdom of God.

"So the kingdom of God is not like you think it is, that God will come to reign over you. God only planted the spirit, and the kingdom of God will only be within those who preserve that. God does not control people and, like a farmer, tosses seeds to the earth and does not think of them himself. The seeds swell on their own, sprout, grow into a plant, a stalk, a head of grain, and then produce a kernel. And only when it is ripe does the farmer send the reapers to mow the field. Just so, God gave the world his son, a spirit, and the spirit will grow in the world and the sons of the spirit will make up the kingdom of God.

"Like a woman who adds yeast to the dough, she mixes it with the flour and then stops kneading it, and waits for it to ferment on its own and rise. While people are still living, God does not enter into their lives; he gave the world the spirit and the spirit itself lives within people, forming the kingdom of God. For the spirit there is no death and no evil. Death and evil are for the flesh and not for the spirit.

"This is what the kingdom of God can be compared to: A farmer sowed good seeds in his field. The farmer is the spirit father; the field is the earth; the good seeds are the sons of the kingdom of God.

"Now, the farmer lay down to sleep and an enemy came to plant weeds in the field. The enemy is temptation, the weeds are the sons of temptation. Then, workers came to the master and said, 'Did you plant bad seeds? Many weeds have turned up in your field. Send us and we will go and clear the field.'

"And the farmer said, 'There is no need; you might begin pulling out the weeds and trample the wheat while doing so. Let them grow together. The harvest will come, then I'll command the reapers to pull out the weeds and will burn them up and will gather the wheat into my shed.'

"The harvest is the end of human life, and the reapers are the powers of heaven. They burn the weeds and the wheat will be cleaned and gathered. Just so, at the end of life, all that was a trick of time will fall away, and only the true life will remain—life in the spirit. For the spirit father there is no evil. The spirit guards what he needs and that which does not come from him, does not exist for him.

"The kingdom of God is like a fishing net. They stretch fishing nets along the sea and catch all kinds of fish. And then, when they pull it out, they separate the rubbish and throw it back into the sea. And so it will be at the end of time: the power of heaven will pick out the good, and the bad will be thrown away."

And as he finished talking, his students began to ask him, "How should we understand these parables?"

And he said to them, "These parables must be understood in two ways. After all, I tell all of these parables because there are some, like you, my students, who partially understand the nature of the kingdom of God, who understand that the kingdom of God is within every person, and understand how to enter into it; and then there are others who do not understand it. Others look, but do not see, and they hear but do not understand, because their hearts have grown fat. Now I tell these parables on two levels, to the one group as well as to the other. To some, I speak of God, of what God considers his kingdom to be, and they can understand that. To you, though, I speak of what the kingdom of God is for you, the one that is within you.

"And pay attention. Understand the parable of the sower as you should. For you, this is what the parable means: Evil comes to everyone who has understood the meaning of the kingdom of God but has not accepted it into his heart: it snatches up what has been sown. This is the seed that fell on the road. The one that was sown on the stones, that is he who immediately accepts with joy. But there is no root within him, and so he only accepts it for a time and then finds restriction and persecution because of the meaning of the kingdom and so he turns away from it. The one sown in the brush, that is he who has understood the meaning of the kingdom, but his worldly cares and greed for riches snuff out the meaning in him and he bears no fruit. And the one sown on good land, that is the one who has understood the meaning of the kingdom and accepted it into his heart. This one bears fruit, some multiplied one hundred times, some sixty, and some thirty. And whoever holds on will be given much; but whoever does not hold on will have everything taken away from him.

"And therefore, be careful how you understand these parables. Understand them so that you do not become ensnared in error, offenses or concerns, but bear fruit thirty times, sixty times, or one hundred times more. In the soul, the kingdom of heaven flourishes out of nothing, but it gives everything. Like a birch seed, the smallest of all seeds, when it grows up, it is larger than all the other trees and the birds of the heavens build their nests in it."

Chapter Four

THE KINGDOM OF GOD

And therefore the will of the father is life and goodness
for all people.

THY KINGDOM COME

*Jesus is sorry for people because they do not know true goodness, so he
teaches them, saying:*

*Those who have no belongings and no glory and are not troubled by this
are blessed; but those who seek riches and glory are unlucky, because in
terms of the father's will they are poor and destitute, seeking only rewards
from people in this temporal life. In order to fulfill the will of the father, one
should not fear being poor and despised, one must rejoice in that state so as
to demonstrate what real goodness is.*

*In order to fulfill the will of the father, who gives life and goodness to all
people, one must keep five commandments.*

*The first commandment: Do not offend anyone and do not do anything
to provoke evil in anyone, because evil gives birth to evil.*

*The second commandment: Do not be charmed by women and do not
abandon the woman that you've united with, because abandoning women
and replacing them gives rise to all the debauchery in the world.*

*The third commandment: Do not swear oaths over anything because it
is impossible to promise anything since man is entirely in the hands of the
father, and oaths are judged as evil acts.*

The fourth commandment: Do not oppose evil, but tolerate insults and do even more than people require of you: do not judge, and you will not be judged. All that man can teach by taking vengeance is vengeance.

The fifth commandment: Do not make distinctions between your homeland and that of others, because all people are the children of one father.

These five commandments should be kept, not to earn the praise of other people, but for yourself, for your own blessedness. Neither prayer nor fasting are necessary. Praying is not necessary because the father knows all that people need. So there is nothing to ask him for; one just needs to try to be within the father's will, not bearing any malice toward anyone. Fasting is not necessary because people fast only for the praise of other people; and the praise of other people cannot give blessedness. The father gives life; he gives his children what they need. One need only worry about being within the father's will at any given moment, the rest will take care of itself.

One can only desire strength of spirit, which is what the father gives. The five commandments define the path into the kingdom of heaven. Only this singularly narrow path leads into eternal life. False teachers, wolves in sheep's clothing, always try to lead people off of this path. One must beware of them. One can always tell a false teacher because they teach evil in the name of good. If they teach violence or punishment, they are false teachers. You can recognize them by the acts which they teach. It is not the one who calls on the name of God that fulfills the will of God, but the one who performs acts of goodness.

So, he who keeps these five commandments will have a life of certainty which no one will be able to take from him, and he who does not keep them will have a life that will be quickly taken from him, so that nothing remains.

Jesus's teaching amazes and attracts all the people because he acknowledges the people's freedom. His teaching is a fulfillment of Isaiah's prophecy about God's chosen one bringing light to people, conquering evil and restoring truth through meekness, humility and goodness—and not through violence.

And Jesus walked from city to village and taught all the people about the blessing of fulfilling the father's will. Jesus felt sorry that they were all perishing, not knowing what true life was, rushing around and tormenting themselves without knowing why, like lambs left unattended by their shepherd.

Once, a crowd of people gathered for Jesus, to hear his teaching, and he went up onto a mountain and sat down. His students surrounded him. And Jesus began to teach the people about the father's will.

He said: "Blessed are the poor and homeless because they live within the will of God. If they go hungry, they will be filled; if they grieve and weep, they will be comforted. If people despise them, avoid them and drive them out, let them take joy in that, because the people of God were always driven out this way. And they will receive their reward from heaven.

"But sorrow to the rich men because they have already received all that they desired and they will not receive anything beyond it. For now they are satisfied, but they will become hungry. Now they are happy, but they will experience sadness. If everyone flatters them, then sorrow to them, because only swindlers flatter people. Blessed are the poor and homeless, but they are only blessed when they are poor not just in appearance, but also in their souls, just as salt can only be good when it does not just look like salt, but also has the qualities of salt through and through. Just so, you, poor and homeless teachers of the world, you are blessed if you know that true happiness is to be found in being homeless and poor. If you are poor only in appearance, then, like unsavory salt, you are not good for much.

"You are light for the world, so do not hide your light, but show it to people. After all, having lit a light, no one puts it under a bench, they put it on the table so that it shines for everyone in the room.

Likewise, you must not hide your light, but you must show it in your actions, so that people can see that you know the truth. And, seeing your good works, they will come to understand your heavenly father.

"And do not think that I am liberating you from the law. I do not teach liberation from the law, but fulfillment of the eternal law. As long as there are people under heaven, there will be an eternal law. The law will only cease to exist when people do everything in and of themselves according to the eternal law. And now I am going to give you the commandments of the eternal law. And if anyone exempts themselves from even one of these short commandments and teaches others that it is possible to exempt themselves from any, he will be the last into the kingdom of heaven; but the one who fulfills the commandments and teaches others to do so also will be great in the kingdom of heaven. Because if your virtue is no more than the virtue of the orthodox scribes, then there is no way that you can be in the kingdom of heaven.

"Here are the commandments:

"*The first commandment.* In the previous law it was said: do not kill. And if anyone kills another, then he must be killed. But I say to you that judgment awaits all who are angry with their brother. And the one who curses at his brother is even more guilty. So, if you want to pray to God, then recall first whether there is any man who may have something to hold against you, and if you recall that even one man considers that you have insulted him, leave your prayers and go first to make peace with your brother, and only then pray. You know that God does not need your sacrifices or your prayers, but he does need peace, agreement and love between you. And you know that it is impossible for you to either pray or think of God if there is even one person with whom you do not share loving feelings. This then is the *first commandment*: Do not be angry, do not curse, and if you have spoken evil words, then make peace and be sure that not one person has cause to be offended by you.

"*The second commandment.* In the previous law it was said: do not commit adultery. And if you want to abandon your wife, then give her divorce papers. But I say to you that if you lust after a woman's beauty then you are already committing adultery. Every type of depravity destroys the soul, so therefore it is better for you to refrain from the comforts of the flesh than to destroy your life. And if you abandon your wife, then, in addition to the fact that you are a philanderer, you also force her into depravity along with whoever subsequently couples with her. Therefore, this is the *second commandment*: Do not think that the love of women is good. Do not desire women, but live with the one you have committed to and do not leave her.

"*The third commandment.* In the previous law it was said: do not take the name of the Lord your God in vain and do not call upon your God falsely. Do not dishonor the name of your God. Do not swear by me dishonestly and thereby desecrate your God. But I say to you that every oath is a desecration of God, so therefore, do not make any oaths. It is impossible for a man to promise anything since he is always entirely under God's power. He cannot make anyone's gray hair black, so how can he make oaths for the future, saying that he will do this or that and swearing by God. Every oath is a desecration of God because if the person is called upon to fulfill an oath that opposes God's will, then it turns out that he has promised to act contrary to God's will. Therefore, every oath is evil. But when you are asked something, say yes, if yes; no, if no, and anything else that you add to that will be evil. And so, this is *the third commandment*: Never make any oaths about anything to anyone. Say yes, when you mean yes; no, when you mean no, and know that every oath is evil.

"*The fourth commandment.* In the previous law it was said: who-ever destroys the soul must repay soul for soul, eye for eye, tooth for tooth, hand for hand, ox for ox, slave for slave and much more. But I say to you: do not fight evil with evil and do not just avoid claiming ox for ox, slave for slave, soul for soul before the courts, but do not oppose evil in any sense. If someone wants to take your ox from you in court, give him another one in addition. If someone wants to sue you in court for your jacket, give him your shirt too. If someone knocks your teeth out from one cheek, turn the other toward him as well. If they force you to take on one job, take on two. If someone takes your belongings, release them freely. If they give you no money, do not ask for any.

"And so: Do not judge and you will not be judged, do not punish and you will not be judged and punished. Forgive others and you will be forgiven, because if you judge people then they will also judge you. You are forbidden from judging, because you, like all people, are blind and do not see truth. With dirt clogging your eyes, how are you going to view the speck of dirt in your brother's eye? First you need to wash out your own eye; but who has clean eyes? Can a blind man lead a blind man? Both will fall into a pit. It is the same with those who judge and punish; they are like the blind lead-ing the blind. Those who judge and condemn to violent punish-ment, wounds, mutilations and death do so because they want to teach people. But what can come of them teaching, other than that the pupil will master the topic and become exactly like the teacher. What will he do when he masters it? Exactly what the teacher does: violence and murder.

"And do not think that you will find justice in the court. Giving your love of justice to a human court is the same as throwing your priceless pearl to the pigs: they will trample it and then tear you to pieces. And so, this is *the fourth commandment*: No matter how they insult you, do not oppose evil, do not judge and you will not be judged; do not make complaints and do not punish.

"*The fifth commandment.* In the previous law it was said: do good to your own people and do harm to the foreigner. But I say to you: love not only your own countrymen, but also the people of other nations. Let others hate you, let them attack you and insult you; but you must praise them and do good to them. If you are only good to your own countrymen, then you are like everyone else who is good to their own countrymen; and it is because of this that wars occur. But you should treat all nations equally, and if you do, you will be the sons of the father. All people are his children, consequently all people should be your brothers. And so, this is *the fifth commandment*: Keep the same law in regard to other nations that I have asked you to keep amongst yourselves. For the father of all people there is no such thing as different nations, there are no different kingdoms either: all are brothers, all are sons of the one father. Don't create differences between people based on nations and kingdoms.

"*Now then*: (1) Do not be angry, but be at peace with all people; (2) Do not amuse yourself with depravity; (3) Do not take oaths for anyone for any reason; (4) Do not resist evil, do not judge and you will not be judged; (5) Do not make distinctions between different nations and love the foreigner as you would your own people.

"All of these commandments are as one: All that you wish people would do for you, do for them. Do not keep these commandments for the praise of people. If you do it for people, then your reward will also be from people. But if it is not for people, then your reward will be from the heavenly father.

"Therefore, if you do good to people, do not trumpet about it in front of people. That is what the deceivers do, so that people praise them. They get what they desire. But if you do good to people, then do it so that no one sees you, so that your left hand does not know what your right hand is doing. And your father will see this and give you what you need.

"And if you want to pray, then do not pray like the deceivers do. The deceivers love to pray in churches, in the sight of other people. They do this for people and because of people, and they get what they desire. But if you want to pray, go to where no one can see you and pray to your spirit father; and the father will see what is in your soul, and will give you what you desire in spirit. Whoever prays should not babble like a performer. Your father knows what you need before you even open your mouth.

"Pray only like this: Our father, without beginning or end, like heaven! Let only your being be holy. Let all power be yours only, so that your will comes to pass without beginning and without end on earth. Give me the food of life in the present. Repair and wipe away my earlier mistakes just as I will repair and wipe away the mistakes of my brothers, so that I do not fall into temptation but will be spared from evil. Because the power and strength is yours and the judgment is yours.

"If you pray, then first of all do not hold a grudge against anyone. And if you do not forgive people their errors, then your father will not forgive you your errors. If you fast, have patience and don't show it off to people; that is what the deceivers do, so that people see them and praise them. And people do praise them, so they receive what they desire. But do not do that; if you are suffering from some need, then go about with a joyful face, so that people do not see, but your father will see this and give you what you need.

"Do not store up supplies on earth. On earth, the worm will chew it, and rust will eat it, and thieves will steal it; but you should store up your heavenly riches. Heavenly riches cannot be chewed by worms or eaten by rust, and they cannot be stolen by thieves. Wherever your treasure is, your heart will also be found there. The eye is light for the body, but the heart is light for the soul. If your eye is dark, then your whole body will be in darkness. And if the light of your heart is dark, then your whole soul will be in darkness. It is impossible to serve two masters simultaneously. You can satisfy one, but you will insult the other. It is impossible to serve God and the flesh. You are either working for earthly life or for God.

"Therefore, do not worry about what you will eat and drink and what you will wear. After all, life is more complex than just food and clothing, and God is the one that gave it to you. Take a look at God's creations, at the birds: they do not sow, they do not reap, they do not gather, and God nourishes them. Before God, man is no worse than a bird. If God gave life to man, then he is capable of keeping man nourished. And after all, you know yourselves that no matter how you exert yourself, you cannot do a thing for yourselves. You cannot lengthen your lives by even one hour.

"And why should you worry about clothing? The flowers of the field do not work and do not spin thread. And they are attired in such a way that even Solomon in all his splendor was never attired. And if God attired this grass that grows today but is cut down tomorrow, then what, will he not dress you too? Do not worry and do not overexert yourself, do not say that we must think about what we'll eat and what we'll wear. All people have these needs and God knows about your needs.

"And so, do not worry about the future. Live for the present day. Worry about being within the father's will. Desire that one important thing and all the rest will come of its own. Just try to be within the father's will.

"And so, do not worry about the future. When the future arrives, there will be enough to worry about then. There is always enough evil in the present.

"Ask, and it will be given to you. Seek and you will find. Knock and it will open up to you.

"Is there such a father that will give his son a stone instead of bread or a snake instead of fish? So then, how could it be that we, evil people, know how to give our children what they need, but your father in heaven would not give you what you truly need when you ask him? Ask, and the heavenly father will give the life of the spirit to those that ask for it. The path to life is narrow, but you should enter by way of this narrow path. There is but one entry into life: it is narrow and tight. And the surrounding field is large and broad, but it leads to ruin. Only the narrow path leads to life; and only a few find it.

"But do not be timid, little flock! The father has reserved the kingdom for us. Only beware of false prophets and teachers; they come to you in sheep skins, but underneath they are predatory wolves. By their fruits, by that which is born from them, you will be able to recognize them. You will never gather grapes from a burdock or apples from an aspen. But a good tree will grow good fruit. And a bad tree will grow bad fruit. And so, by the fruit of their teaching you can recognize them.

"A good man produces only good things from his good heart. But an evil man produces evil things from his evil heart, because the mouth speaks from the heart's abundance. And therefore, if the teachers teach you to do to other people what would be harmful to do to yourself—if, for example, they teach violence, punishment, or war—know that they are false teachers. Because it is not the one who says 'Lord, Lord!' that enters the kingdom of heaven, but he who does the will of the heavenly father. They will say, 'Lord! Lord! We taught according to your teaching and we forced out evil by means of your teaching.'

"But I turn away from them and say to them, 'No, I never claimed you and do not claim you now. Get away from me: you are doing iniquity.'

"And so, whoever may be hearing these commandments of mine—do not be angry, do not philander, do not make oaths, do not resist evil, do not differentiate your people from others—whoever hears them and keeps them is an intelligent person and builds his home on a rock. And his home will withstand all storms. And whoever hears these commandments and does not keep them is like the stupid person who builds his home on sand. As soon as the storm comes, the home will fall and everyone will perish."

And all the people were amazed at this because Jesus's teaching was completely different than the teaching of the orthodox legalists. The orthodox legalists taught a law that had to be obeyed; but Jesus taught that all people are free.

And the prophecy of Isaiah was fulfilled in Jesus: That the people who were living in darkness, in the shadow of death, saw the light of life and that he who brought the light of truth would do no harm or violence to people, but that he would be meek and humble. That he, in order to bring light into the world, would not quarrel, would not shout, that no one would ever hear him raise his voice. That he would not break the reed and not blow out the night light. And that all of the people's hope would hinge on his teaching.

Chapter Five

TRUE LIFE

The satisfaction of personal will leads to death, the
satisfaction of the father's will gives true life.

THY WILL BE DONE

*Wisdom consists of recognizing one's own life as a son of the spirit father.
People give themselves goals in mortal life and as they work to achieve
these goals, they torment themselves and others. When they accept the
teaching about the life of the spirit and submit and humble themselves in
the flesh, people find complete satisfaction in the life of the spirit, the life
that has been allotted them.*

*Jesus asks a woman of another faith for a drink. She denies him on the
pretext of their differing faith. Jesus says to her, "If you understood that a
living man is asking you for a drink, one in whom the spirit of the father resides, then you would not deny the request, but would seek to do me good,
and thereby unite in spirit with the father."*

*Jesus says to his students, "A person's true food is to fulfill the will of
the spirit father. Fulfilling his will is always possible. Our entire life is
the gathering of the fruits of life, which the father has planted within us.
Fruits are the good acts that we do to other people. One must never cease to
live and do good to people."*

*In Jerusalem there is a bathhouse at which a sick man lays, doing noth-
ing, waiting for a miracle healing. Jesus approaches the weak man, saying,
"Do not await a miracle healing, but go and live, with as much strength
as you have in yourself and do not mistake the meaning of life." The weak*

man obeys Jesus, stands and walks off. The orthodox reproach Jesus because he had raised a feeble man on the Sabbath. Jesus says to them, "I did nothing new. I simply did what our mutual spirit father does. He lives and animates people. And that is every person's calling. Every person is free and can either choose to live, doing the will of the father and doing good to others, or not to live, doing their own will and not doing good to others.

"People's true lives are like this: A master gives his slaves a portion of his priceless estate and commands each to labor over the part that he gave them. Some work, others do not, hiding what was given to them. When the master makes his account, he gives to those that worked an even bigger measure of what they had, and from those that did not work he takes away all that they had been given. This is like the spirit of life within a person—he who works for the spirit of life receives endless life, he who does not work loses the one that has been given to him. The only true life is the life that is common to all, and not the life of a single person. All people should work for the life of others."

Jesus's disciples do not know how to feed the crowd that has followed him into the wilderness. Jesus asks that all available bread be given to him. He takes the bread, gives it to his apostles, they give it to the others and the others begin to do the same. All the people eat at someone else's hands and they are all satisfied together, yet there is food remaining. Jesus says, "It is unnecessary for everyone to obtain food for themselves. Give others something to eat—that is what the spirit within man dictates. Man's real food is the spirit of the father. You should serve all life, since life is not a matter of doing one's own will, but the will of the father of life. The father, the source of all life, is a spirit. Life is just the fulfillment of the father's will and so, in order to fulfill the spirit's will, one must give up the flesh. The flesh becomes food for the life of the spirit. Only by yielding our flesh do we allow the spirit to live."

Jesus selects certain of his students and sends them to preach the life of the spirit. As he sends them off, he says, "To preach the life of the spirit you *must renounce all lusts of the flesh and must not possess anything of your own. Be prepared for persecutions, deprivations and sufferings. You will be hated by those who love mortal life. They will torment and murder you, but do not be afraid. If you do the father's will, then you will have the life of the spirit, which no one can take from you."*

When the students return, they announce that they have defeated evil teachings everywhere they have gone. The orthodox contend that if his teaching defeated evil, then it must be evil itself, since people must endure suffering when they follow it. To this, Jesus says, "Evil cannot defeat evil. If evil is victorious, then it only conquers with goodness. Goodness is the will of the spirit father, who is common to all people. Everyone knows that goodness exists for themselves, and if they perform their actions for other people and do the will of the spirit father, then they do good. And therefore, fulfilling the spirit father's will is good, though it may be yoked with suffering and death for those who fulfill it."

And Jesus rejoiced deeply over the power of the spirit and said, "I recognize the father's spirit as the source of all things in heaven and on earth because what has been hidden from the clever and the wise ones is now opening to the uneducated simply because they see themselves as sons of the father.

"All people worry about the well-being of the flesh, they have loaded up a kind of cart that they could never pull away; they have placed a yoke on themselves which was not designed to fit them. Understand my teaching and follow it, and you will come to know peace and joy in life. I will give you a different yoke and a different cart: spiritual life. Harness yourselves to it and you will learn calmness and blessedness from me. Be peaceful and meek in heart and you will find blessedness in your life. Because my teaching is a yoke designed to fit you; fulfilling my teaching is an easy cart to pull and a yoke designed to fit you."

Once, Jesus went into the city of the Samaritan Sychar near the field that Jacob gave to his son Joseph. And the well of Jacob was there. Jesus was tired from the road and he sat down at the well.

And a woman of Samaria came for water and Jesus said to her, "Give me something to drink."

And Jesus's students went into the city to buy some food.

And the Samaritan woman said to him, "How can you, a Jew, ask me for a drink? After all, Jews do not associate with Samaritans."

And Jesus said to her, "If you understood what God has given people and who it is that asks you for a drink, I would give you the water of life."

And the woman said, "You don't even have a bucket and the well is very deep. How will you give me the water of life? Are you greater than our father Jacob? He gave this well as a gift and drank from it himself, as did his children and livestock."

And Jesus answered, "Whoever drinks his fill of this water will again become thirsty, but whoever drinks his fill of the water that I will give will never again know thirst. But the water that I give will produce in him a fountain of water flowing into eternal life."

And the woman said, "Give me that kind of water, so that it will no longer be necessary to drink or come to the well for water."

And Jesus said, "Go call your husband and come back here."

And the woman said, "I see that you are a prophet. Our fathers here pray to God on this mountain, but you say that the place of God, where one ought to pray, is in Jerusalem."

And Jesus said to her, "Believe me, woman, people do not pray to the father either here on this mountain or in Jerusalem. The time has come for people to pray authentically, to the father of life in both spirit and in action. These are the kind of worshippers that the father needs. The father is a spirit and he must be prayed to in spirit and in action."

And the woman said, "I know that the messiah is coming, and when he does, he will tell us everything."

And Jesus said, "I am telling you everything."

And the woman went and called the people.

At that moment, the students returned with bread and asked Jesus whether he would like to eat.

And he said, "I have food that you know nothing about."

They thought that someone had brought him something to eat.

But he said, "My food is to do the will of the one who gave me life and to accomplish that which he has entrusted to me. Do not say, 'There is still time,' as the plowman says, waiting for the harvest. He who does the will of the father will always be full and will know neither hunger nor thirst. Fulfilling the will of God always satisfies a person, it carries its own reward. One cannot say, 'I will do the father's will later.' As long as there is life, it will always be both possible and necessary to fulfill the father's will. Our life is a field that God planted; and our task is to gather his fruit. And if we gather fruit then we receive a reward: life outside of time. It is true that we do not give ourselves life, but that someone else gives it. And if we labor to gather this life, then we, like the reapers, will receive a reward. I am teaching you to gather this life that the father has given to you."

Once, Jesus came to Jerusalem. And at that time there was a bathhouse in Jerusalem. Concerning this bathhouse, people said that an angel would descend into it and that the water in the pool would subsequently begin to froth, and that whoever would be the first to plunge into the pool after the water froths up would be healed of whatever sickness he had. And an awning had been made near the bathhouse. And under this awning the sick lay and waited for the water to froth up in the bathhouse and then to plunge in.

And a man was there, debilitated in his ailment for thirty-eight years. Jesus asked him what he was doing. The man related that he had been ill for thirty-eight years and was still waiting to be the first into the bath after the water froths up, so that he could be healed, but that for thirty-eight years he had not been able to get in first, that all the others got into the water before him to bathe.

And Jesus saw that he was old and said, "Do you want to recover?"

And the man said, "I want to, but I don't have anyone to carry me into the water on time. Somebody always gets in before me."

And Jesus said to him, "Wake up, take your bed and go."

And the weak man took his bed and walked off. And it was on the Sabbath.

And the orthodox said, "You cannot carry your bed off today, it is the Sabbath."

He said, "The one who raised me commanded me to take the bed with me."

The invalid went off and told the orthodox that Jesus had healed him. And the orthodox grew angry and persecuted Jesus because he had taken such action on the Sabbath.

And Jesus said, "Whatever the father always does, I do as well. I tell the truth to you: the son can do nothing in and of himself. He can only do what he has understood from the father. What the father does is what he does. The father loves the son and because of this he taught the son all that he must do. The father gives life to the dead, and likewise, the son gives life to those he wants to give it to; since the father's business is life, the son's business should likewise be life. The father did not condemn people to death, but gave people power according to their will, either to die or to live. And they will live if they respect the son as they do the father.

"I tell you truly: whoever has understood the meaning of my teaching and has come to believe in the common father of all people already has life and is delivered from death. Those who understood the meaning of human life have already left death behind and will live forever. Because just as the father lives independently in and of himself, just so, he planted life in the son himself. And he gave him freedom. Because of this, he is the son of man.

"From now on, all mortals are divided into two groups. Only those that do good find life; and those that do evil will be destroyed. And this is not my judgment, but just what I have come to understand from the father. But my judgment is correct because I judge these things not in order to do what I want, but so that everyone does what the father of all wants. If I convinced everyone that my teaching is true, then that would not prove my teaching. But there is something that proves my teaching—the actions that I teach. They show that I do not teach from myself, but from the father of all people. And my father, the one that taught me, he confirms within the souls of all people the truth of my commandments. But you do not want to understand and know his voice. And you do not hold on to the meaning of this voice. You do not believe that you have a spirit within you, a spirit that has come down from heaven.

"Give some thought to the meaning of your scriptures. You will find the same substance in them as in my teaching. They are commandments about how to live for more than just yourself, how to do good to all people. I teach you in the name of the common father of all people, and you do not accept my teaching, but if someone teaches you in their own name, you believe that. You should not believe in what people say to one another, you should only believe that the son is within every person, and that the son is the same as the father."

And so that people would not think that the heavenly kingdom was a visible phenomenon, so that they would understand that the kingdom of God is simply the fulfilling of the father's will and that the fulfilling of the father's will depends on the strength of every person, and so that all people would understand that life is not given to each person for their individual use, but to fulfill the father's will and that only the fulfilling of the father's will can save from death and give life, Jesus told a parable.

He said, "There was a rich man who needed to leave his home. Before his departure, he called his servants and distributed ten talents, one for each, and he said to them, 'While I am absent, each of you must work with what I have given you.'

"But it happened that when he left, a few residents of this city said, 'We don't want to serve him any longer.'

"And so, when the rich man returned from his absence, he called these servants to whom he had given money and commanded them each to report what they had done with his money.

"The first came and said, 'Look, master, I made ten out of the one that you gave me.'

"And the master said to him, 'Good, you good servant, you were loyal in a small matter, I will place you in charge of large matters, you will be one with me in all my riches.'

"Another servant came and said, 'Look, master, I made five from the one talent.'

"And the master said to him, 'You have done well, good servant, be one with me in all my possessions.'

"One more came and said, 'Here is the talent that you gave me. I hid it in a handkerchief and buried it. I did so because I was afraid of you. You are a severe man: you withdraw from where you made no deposit and gather where you did not sow.'

"And the master said to him, 'You foolish servant! I will judge you by your own words. You say that you hid your talent in the earth and did not work with it because you fear me. If you knew that I am severe and that I withdraw from where I have not deposited, then why did you not do as I commanded you to do? If you had worked with my talent, my estate would have grown and you would have fulfilled what I had commanded you to do. But now you have not done the thing for which I gave you the talent, and therefore, you cannot possess it.'

"And the master commanded that the talent be taken from the one that did not work with it and he gave it to the one that worked the most.

"And then the servants said to him, 'Lord, they already have so much.'

"And the master said, 'Give it to them that worked most, because the one who watches over what he has been given will receive even more, and he who does not watch over it will have even his last bit taken away. Drive out the ones who do not want to be under my power, so that they are no longer here.'"

The master—that is the source of life, the spirit father. His servants are people. Talents are the life of the spirit. Just as the master does not work on his estate himself, but commands the servants to work, each on his own, likewise, the spirit of the father placed the spirit of life in people, gave them a decree to work for the life of other people and then left them alone. Those who sent word that they no longer recognize the authority of the master, these are the ones who do not recognize the spirit of life. The return of the master and the demand for the account is the destruction of mortal life and the deciding of people's fates: do they have any other life beyond the one that was given them, or not. Some of the servants, those that fulfill the master's will, work on what was given them and increase the money that they started with, these are the people who, having received life, understand that life is the father's will and that it should serve the life of others. The stupid and evil servant who hid his talent and did not work on it represents those who only fulfill their own will, not the father's will, and do not serve the lives of others. The servants that fulfill the master's will and work for the prosperity of the master's estate become full participants in the master's estate and the servants that do not fulfill his will and do not work for the master are deprived of all that had been previously given. People who fulfill the father's will and serve life become participants in the life of the father and receive life, despite the destruction of mortal life. Those who do not fulfill his will and do not serve life are deprived of the life they had, and they are destroyed. Those that did not want to recognize the master's power do not exist for the master; he banishes them. People who do not recognize the life of the spirit within themselves do not exist for the father.

After this, Jesus went into a deserted place and many people followed after him. And he climbed up onto a mountain and sat there with his students.

And he saw that many people were coming and he said, "Where could we get some bread to feed all of these people?"

Philip said, "Two hundred dinari would not buy enough, even if we gave just a little bit to each person. We have only a little bread and fish."

And another student said, "They have bread, I saw a boy with five loaves of bread and two fish."

And Jesus said, "Tell them all to lie down on the grass." And Jesus took the bread that he had and gave it to his students and commanded them to give it to the others, and thus, everyone began to give what they had to one another, and everyone was filled and much bread was left over.

On the next day, the people came to Jesus again and he said to them, "Now you come to me not because you have seen miracles, but because you ate bread and were filled."

And he said to them, "Do not work for perishable food, but for eternal food, which only the spirit of the son of man can give, sealed by God."

And the Jews said, "What do we need to do in order to perform the acts of God?"

And Jesus said, "The acts of God are based on believing in the life he has given you."

They said, "Give us proof so that we can believe in you and in what you are doing. Our fathers ate manna in the desert. God gave them bread from heaven to eat, so it is written."

Jesus answered them, "The true bread of heaven is the spirit of the son of man, the one that is given by the father, because a person's nourishment comes from the spirit as it descends from heaven. That is what gives life to the world. My teaching gives true nourishment to people. Whoever follows after me will not go hungry, and whoever believes my teaching will never know thirst.

"But I have already told you that you have seen this and you still do not believe. All the life that was given to the son by the father has a place in my teaching and everyone who believes in it will be a participant in it. Because I have come down from heaven not to do whatever I might want, but to do the will of the father, the one who gave me life. The will of the father who sent me is that anyone who sees the son and believes in him will have eternal life."

The Jews were confused by this statement, that his teaching had come down from heaven.

They said, "But this is Jesus, the son of Joseph, we know his father and mother. How is it that he says his teaching has come down from heaven?"

And Jesus said to them, "Do not base your judgments on who I am or where I come from. My teaching is true, not because I plan on convincing you that God spoke with me on Sinai, as Moses did; my teaching is true because it is within you also. And in the prophets it is written that all things will be taught by God. Everyone who comes to understand the father and learns to understand his will becomes devoted to my teaching in the process. No one has ever seen God and no one will, but he who comes from God has seen and continues to see the father.

"He who believes me has eternal life. My teaching is life's nourishment. Your fathers ate manna, food directly from heaven, but they still died. But life's true nourishment, descending from heaven, is such that whoever is nourished by it will not die. My teaching is life's nourishment, descending from heaven. Whoever is nourished by it will live forever. And this nourishment that I am teaching is my flesh, which I surrender for the life of all people."

The Jews did not understand at all what he had said and they began to argue about how one could give up their flesh for the nourishment of other people and why they would do such a thing.

And Jesus said to them, "If you do not give up your flesh for the life of the spirit then there will be no life within you. Whoever does not give up his flesh for the life of the spirit does not have an actual life. The only living part of me is that which surrenders the flesh for the spirit. And therefore, our flesh is the true food for actual life. Only the part of me that consumes my body and gives up mortal life for true life, only this part is me, the true me. It is within me, and I am within it. And just as I live in the flesh by the will of the father, that which lives within me lives by my will."

And a few of the students, having heard this, said, "These words are severe, and it is hard to understand them."

And Jesus said to them, "You are so confused that what I am saying to you seems difficult, even though it concerns what man always has been, is and what he always will be. Man is a spirit in the flesh, and only the spirit gives life, the flesh does not give life. Though I used words that seemed sharp to you, I have said nothing more, after all, than that the spirit is life."

Then Jesus chose seventy people from his close followers and sent them to the places that he wanted to be himself.

He told them, "Many people do not know the blessing of real life. I am sorry for all of them and I want to teach them all. But just as the master is not enough to perform the harvest of his whole field alone, I also cannot do this alone.

"Go to the various cities and announce everywhere the fulfillment of the will of God. Say that the will of the father is in the five commandments: the first—do not be angry, the second—do not be depraved, the third—do not swear oaths, the fourth—do not resist evil and the fifth—do not create divisions between people. And so, moreover, keep these commandments in all things yourselves. I send you to go like lambs among wolves. Be wise like snakes and pure like doves.

"First of all, do not possess anything, do not take anything with you: no bag, no bread, no money, only your garment for your body and shoes. Then, do not create divisions between people, do not choose only the masters at the places you stop. But whatever home you happen to enter first, stay in the same one. When you come into the home, greet the masters. If they take you in, stay; if they do not take you in, go to the next house. You will be hated greatly, attacked and driven out for what you say. And when they drive you out, you must go to another village, and when they drive you out of that one, go to yet another. They will pursue you, like wolves pursue sheep. But do not be timid. Endure until the final hour.

"And they will take you to court and judge you, they will whip you, and they will take you to their leaders and force you to defend yourselves to them. And when they take you to court, do not be timid and do not plan out what to say: the spirit of the father will tell you internally what you ought to say.

"You will not manage to get to all cities before their people come into contact with your teaching and are converted to it. So do not be afraid. What is hidden in people's souls will come out into the open. What you say to two or three will be spread out among thousands.

"The main thing is to not be afraid of those that can kill your body: they cannot do anything to your souls. So do not be afraid of them. Just be afraid of how your body and soul may be destroyed. If you fall away from fulfilling the will of the father, that is what you should fear. Sparrows are sold five to the kopeck, but they do not die without the father willing it. And no hair will fall from your head without the father's will. So what have you to be afraid of if you are within the father's will?

"Not everyone will believe in my teaching. And those that do not believe will hate it because it deprives them of what they love, and there will be contention. My teaching, like fire, will ignite the world. And contention will arise from this in the world. Contention will arise in every home. Family members will come to hate those who accept my teaching, father will contend with son, mother with daughter. And they will kill them. Because for him who understands my teaching, these things will no longer have any meaning: not father, not mother, not wife, not children, not any of his belongings."

And then the orthodox scholars came from Jerusalem and approached Jesus. Jesus was located in a certain village and a multitude of people had crowded into the house and was standing all around. The orthodox began to speak to the people to prevent them from listening to the teaching of Jesus, they said that Jesus was possessed and that if one were to live by his commandments more evil would exist among the people than currently did. They said that he was casting out evil with evil.

Jesus called to them, saying, "You say that I am casting out evil with evil. But no force can use itself to destroy itself. If it could destroy itself this way, then it simply would not exist. You cast out evil with threats, punishments, and murders yet, despite your efforts, evil is still not destroyed, namely because it cannot attack itself. But

I cast out evil differently than you do, to be precise, without using evil. I cast out evil by calling people to fulfill the will of the spirit father, the one who gives life to all. The five commandments express the will of the spirit, the one who brings goodness and life.

"And therefore the commandments destroy evil. And that is proof to you that they are true. If people were not sons of one spirit, it would be impossible to conquer evil, just as it is impossible to go into a strong man's house and rob him. In order to rob the home of a strong man, you must first bind the strong man securely.

"People are bound like this by the unity of the spirit of life. For this reason, I tell you that every human mistake and every misrepresentation will not be held against you; but misrepresentation of the holy spirit, which gives life to all, will not be forgiven. If someone says a word against a person, it is nothing; but if a person says something against that which is holy within a person, against the spirit, then it cannot be taken lightly. You can reproach me as you like, but do not call those life commandments that I have revealed to you evil.

"One must be either together with the spirit of life or against it. One must serve the spirit of life and goodness in all people, and not just in oneself alone. Either you consider that life and blessedness is good for the whole world, and as a result you love life and blessedness for all people, or you consider life and blessedness to be evil, and as a result you will not love life and blessedness even in yourself; either you consider a tree to be good and its fruit good or you consider the tree to be bad and its fruit bad. Because a tree is valued by the quality of its fruit."

Chapter Six

FALSE LIFE

And therefore, in order to receive true life,
Man must renounce the false mortal life on earth
and live by the spirit.

ON EARTH AS IT IS IN HEAVEN

For the life of the spirit there can be no difference between family and strangers. Jesus says that his mother and brothers mean nothing to him as family, but that only those who do the will of the common father are close to him. The ones who hold to the understanding of the father are blessed.

Jesus says that he does not have a specific place for himself, since he lives by the spirit. Living by the father's will is possible in all places and at all times. The death of the flesh cannot be frightening for a person who has given themselves up to the father's will because the life of the spirit is not dependent on the death of the flesh. Jesus says that whoever believes in the life of the spirit cannot fear anything.

In response to the man who says he will fulfill Jesus's teachings afterwards, but that first he must bury his father, Jesus answers, "Only the dead should worry about burying the dead; those who live always live by fulfilling the will of the father." Concerns about family and domestic duties cannot disturb the life of the spirit. Whoever worries about what will become of his mortal life as a result of fulfilling the father's will does the same as the plowman who plows looking backward instead of forward. Concerns about the joys of mortal life, which seem so important to people, are like a dream. The only actions in life that are real are proclaiming the father's will, attending to it and fulfilling it.

To Martha's reproach about how she alone is concerned with dinner while her sister Mary does not help her, but sits listening to the teaching, Jesus says, "Worry about the worrisome if you must, but leave those who have no need for the flesh to do the one thing that is truly needed in life."

Jesus says that whoever wants to receive true life should first renounce his own personal desires. Such a person should not only refrain from arranging his life according to his own desires so as not to damage the true life of fulfilling the father's will but he must also be ready at any moment to endure all kinds of deprivations and suffering. There are no benefits to be obtained from mortal life if the obtaining of it damages the life of the spirit.

More than anything else, the life of the spirit is damaged by the acquiring of riches. People forget that no matter how many riches and belongings they acquire, they could still die at any moment and having things becomes superfluous. Death is an unavoidable condition of life, it hangs over each of us—sickness, murder at the hands of others, and accidents may cut a life short at any second. If a person is living, then he should look at every hour of his life as a reprieve. We are capable of knowing and predicting all that happens on earth and in heaven, but we forget that death awaits us at any second. If we keep from forgetting that, then we will keep from devoting ourselves to mortal life.

Like the guests who cannot attend the rich man's feast because they are too busy with occupational and family matters, people become distracted by the concerns of mortal life, and deprive themselves of true life. Whoever does not renounce all the cares and fears of mortal life cannot fulfill the father's will since it is impossible to serve yourself partially and the father partially. One must consider, is there any benefit to serving my own flesh, can I arrange my life the way that I want it? One must do the same as the man who is building a house or preparing for war. He calculates whether he can complete construction or whether he can conquer his enemy. And *if he sees that he can't, then of course he does not waste his labors or his soldiers pointlessly. One must calculate the benefits of serving mortal life and one's own will versus the benefits of fulfilling the father's will. Whoever calculates this will not resent forgoing the supposed blessedness and supposed life of mortality in order to receive true blessedness and true life. Since it is impossible to arrange life according to your desires, it is better to leave all flesh behind and serve the spirit. Otherwise you will have neither one nor the other. You will not be able to manage mortal life and you will lose the life of the spirit.*

Like the estate manager who is aware that his master may dismiss him at any time, and so does good to other people while still in charge of the master's riches, ensuring that when he is eventually dismissed he will be taken in and cared for, people should remember that mortal life is wealth that belongs to someone else, and that they manage it only temporarily. If they wisely use this other person's wealth, then they'll receive their own true wealth. If we do not give up our false property, then true property will never belong to us. The rich man is already guilty because he eats his fill and does so extravagantly while poor people are going hungry at his doors. Possessions which are not shared with others are nothing but the unfulfilled will of the father.

An orthodox believer, a wealthy leader of men, comes to Jesus, boasting that he has fulfilled all the commandments in the law. Jesus reminds him that there is a commandment to love all people as yourself, and that this is what the father's will is based on. This leader says that he has done that as well. Jesus responds, "That is not true. If you wanted to fulfill the father's will, you would have no possessions. It is impossible to fulfill the father's will if you have your own belongings . . . People assume that without possessions it would be impossible to live; but I say to you that true life consists of giving what is yours to others."

One man, Zacchaeus, hears Jesus's teaching and comes to believe in it. He invites Jesus to his home, and says to him, "I am giving half of my estate to the poor and am repaying four times over everyone that I have ever of-fended." And Jesus says, "Here is a man fulfilling the will of the father. Our whole life must be a sustained act of fulfilling the father's will."

A woman cries to Jesus and fervently pours three hundred rubles' worth of oil on his feet. Judas says that she has done a stupid thing, that she could have fed many people with this money. But Judas was thinking about the benefits of the flesh, not thinking of the poor. Utility is not vital, neither is quantity, but fulfilling, every minute, the father's will, that is what is vital. It is impossible to measure goodness. The widow who gives away her last mite gives more than the rich man who gives thousands. It is also impossible to measure goodness by what is useful and what is not useful.

And once, Jesus's mother and brothers came to him but they could not make contact with Jesus because there were so many people surrounding him.

One man observed them and approached Jesus and said, "Your family members, mother and brothers are standing outside and they want to see you."

And Jesus said, "My mother and brothers are those who have understood the father's will and are fulfilling it."

And a certain woman said, "Blessed is the womb that carried you and the nipples that you sucked."

To this, Jesus said, "Blessed only are those who have understood the knowledge of the father and are keeping it."

And a certain man said to Jesus, "I will follow you no matter where you go."

At this, Jesus said to him, "There is nowhere to follow me. I have no home, no place where I could live. Only animals have lairs and dens, but man is at home anywhere that he can live by the spirit."

And it happened once that Jesus needed to travel by boat with his students.

He said, "We'll go across to the other side."

A storm arose on the lake and began to fill their boat with water so that soon it was on the verge of sinking. And he lay on the deck and slept.

They woke him and said, "Teacher! Do you really not care that we are going to perish?"

And when the storm had grown quiet, he said, "How is it that you are so timid? You have no faith in the life of the spirit within you."

Jesus said to a certain man, "Follow me." And the man said, "I have an elderly father; allow me first to bury him, then I will follow you."

And Jesus said to him, "Let the dead bury the dead, but you, if you want to be alive, fulfill the father's will and proclaim it."

Yet another man said, "I want to be your student and I will fulfill the father's will, as you command, but let me first arrange matters at home."

And Jesus said to him, "If a plowman looks backward, then he cannot plow. No matter how much you look backward, you cannot plow while doing so. One must forget about everything, except for the furrow he is digging. Only then can he plow. If you are pondering how it will affect your mortal life, then you haven't understood the true life and so you cannot live it."

After this, it happened once that Jesus and his students stopped by a certain village. And a certain woman, Martha, invited him into her home. And Martha had a sister named Mary who sat at Jesus's feet and listened to his teaching, while Martha was bustling about making sure that there would be good refreshments.

And Martha approached Jesus and said, "Why don't you do

anything about the fact that my sister has left me all alone to do the serving? Tell her to give me some help."

And in answer, Jesus said, "Martha, Martha, you trouble yourself and are bustling about over many tasks, but there is only one real task required here, and Mary has chosen that required task, one which no one will take from her. Only spiritual food is necessary for life."

And Jesus said to all, "Whoever wants to follow after me, let him renounce his own will and let him be prepared for all types of deprivations and suffering in the flesh, at every hour; only then can he follow after me. Because whoever wants to trouble themselves over their mortal lives will destroy their true life. And if it happens that someone destroys their mortal life while fulfilling the father's will, they will preserve their true life. But what benefit is it to a person if they acquire the whole world but destroy or damage their own life?"

And Jesus said, "Beware of wealth because your life does not hinge on whether you may possess more than others.

"There was a rich man and he was blessed with an abundance of grain.

"And he thought to himself, 'Let me build up the granaries. I will build some big ones and gather all of my wealth there. And I will say to my soul: There you are, soul, there is plenty—rest, eat, drink and live in pleasure.'

"And God said to him, 'You fool, tonight your soul will be taken, and all that you have stored up will be left to someone else.'

"It will be the same with everyone who makes preparations for mortal life and does not live within God."

And Jesus said to them, "Behold, you tell the story of how Pilate put some Galileans to death. But what, were those Galileans really any worse than other people? Is that why this happened to them?

Not at all. We are all like them and we will all perish like them if we do not find salvation from death.

"Or those eighteen men crushed by the tower that collapsed, were they that exceptionally worse than all the other inhabitants of Jerusalem? Not at all. If we do not save ourselves from death, then surely if not now, then tomorrow we will die.

"If we still have not perished, like they have, then we ought to be thinking the following to ourselves: A man has an apple tree growing in his garden. The master comes into the garden, takes a look at the apple tree and sees that there is no fruit on it.

"So the master says to the gardener, 'I have been visiting now for three years and this apple tree is still bare. It must be cut down, otherwise it is just taking up space for nothing.'

"But the gardener says: 'Let us wait a while longer, master, let me dig around it, give it fertilizer, and then we will take a look at it after the summer. Maybe it will bear fruit. And if it doesn't bear fruit all summer, well, then we will cut it down.'

"It is the same with us; while we live by the flesh and do not bear the fruit of spirit life, we are also like a fruitless apple tree. We are left alone for one more summer thanks only to someone else's mercy. But if we do not bear fruit, we will perish just the same as the one who built the granary, just like the Galileans, just like the eighteen crushed by the tower and like all those who do not bear fruit, dying an eternal death.

"No special wisdom is required to understand this; anyone can see it for themselves. After all, we have the power to judge for ourselves and predict not only domestic events, but also what occurs throughout the whole world. If the wind comes from the west, we say, 'It is going to rain.' And so it does. And if the wind comes from the south we say, 'It will be a clear day.' And so it is.

"So, we are capable of predicting the weather, but we fail to predict this other event, that we will all die and perish and that the only salvation for us is the life of the spirit, in fulfilling the will of the spirit."

And many people went with Jesus and again, he said to all of them:

"Whoever wants to be my student, let him esteem fathers, mothers, wives, children, brothers, sisters and all his belongings as nothing and let him be ready for anything at any time. And only the one who does what I do, he alone is following my teaching and he alone is saving himself from death.

"Because everyone, before they undertake anything, considers whether what they are doing is worthwhile, and if it is worthwhile, then they do it; if it is not worthwhile, they give it up. Everyone who builds a house sits down beforehand, of course, and calculates: how much money is needed, how much they have, and whether there is enough to finish the job. They do this to avoid a situation in which they have begun to build but cannot finish and so people laugh at them. Likewise, whoever wants to live their mortal life should calculate beforehand whether they can complete the thing they are working for.

"And every king who wants to go to war thinks first whether he can go to war with ten thousand against an opponent with twenty thousand. If his calculations say that he cannot, then he sends ambassadors and makes peace and no longer prepares for battle. Likewise, before devoting himself to his mortal life, let every man think: Can he do battle against death? Or is it stronger than he is? And in that case, would it not be better to make peace beforehand? Likewise, each of you must first deal with the things that you consider your own: family, money, the estate. And when you determine what use they are, and you realize that they are of no use at all, only then can you be my student."

And having heard this, one man said, "It would be good if there really is a life of the spirit. Otherwise, what if we gave up everything and it turned out that this life did not exist?"

To this, Jesus said, "False. Everyone knows the life of the spirit. You all know that fulfilling the father's will gives life. You know that, but you do not do it, and not because you doubt, but because you are distracted from true life by false cares and you talk your way out of it.

"This is what you do: The master had prepared a meal and sent invitations to his guests, but the guests all began to decline the invitations.

"One said, 'I have bought some land, I must go inspect it.'

"Another said, 'I have bought some bulls, I must take care of them.'

"The third said, 'I have just gotten married and must have a wedding.'

"And the workers came and told the master that no one would be coming. The master then sent his workers out to call the poor. The poor did not decline the invitation and came. When they had all arrived, there was still room.

"And the master sent out again to call people to the meal, saying, 'Go and convince everyone to come to my house for the meal, so that there are more people here.' But those that had refused because they had no time still did not come to the meal. Everyone knows that fulfilling the father's will gives life, but they do not go to the meal because they are distracted by the delusion of wealth.

"Whoever gives up false, temporary wealth for the true life within the father's will does the same as a clever estate manager.

"There was a man who was the estate manager for a wealthy master, and the estate manager saw that the master would soon be turning him out and that he would soon be left with no bread and no shelter.

"And the estate manager thought to himself, 'Here is what I will do: I will distribute from the master's store little by little among the local residents. I will ease their debts, and then, if the master turns me out, the locals will remember my kindness and will not abandon me.'

"And so the estate manager did just that: he called the locals, those that were in debt to the master, and wrote out vouchers for them. For him who was in debt for one hundred, he wrote a voucher for fifty; for him who was in debt for sixty, he wrote one for twenty; and for the others as well.

"And now, the master found out about this and said to himself, 'What is this? He has done something truly clever. Otherwise he would have had to face the world alone. He produced a surplus for me and acted very intelligently with the accounts.'

"In mortal life we all understand what makes an account correct, but as it concerns the life of the spirit we do not want to understand. We must act similarly in regard to unclean and false wealth. We must give it away in order to receive the life of the spirit. And if we are hesitant to give up such meaningless things as wealth for the life of the spirit, it will never be given to us. If we do not give away our false wealth, then likewise, our own individual lives will not be given to us. It is impossible to serve two lords at one time: God and wealth, the will of the father and your own will. It must be either one or the other."

And the orthodox believers heard this. But the orthodox loved wealth, and they laughed at Jesus.

But he said to them, "Do you think that because people respect you for your money, you are actually respectable? No, God does not look at the exterior, he looks at the heart. What people consider unassailable is nothing but vomit before God. Now the kingdom of heaven is on the earth, and those that enter it are great. But the wealthy do not enter it, only those who have nothing can enter.

And it always has been that way, according to your law, according to Moses, and according to all the prophets.

"Listen to how the wealthy and the poor exist, according to your own law:

"There was a rich man. He dressed nicely, strolled around, celebrated every day. And the vagrant Lazarus was covered in scabs.

"And Lazarus came to the rich man's courtyard, thinking, 'Maybe there are some scraps of food left over from this rich man.' But Lazarus was unable to get any scraps because the rich man's dogs had eaten everything up. They also licked Lazarus's wounds.

"And they both died—Lazarus and the rich man. And now, in hell, the rich man saw far, far off that Abraham was seated with the scab-covered Lazarus at his side.

"And the rich man said, 'Lord Abraham, there the scab-covered Lazarus sits with you. He used to wallow at the gate in my courtyard. I do not dare disturb you. But please send scab-covered Lazarus to me and let him dip one finger in water and give me a drop for refreshment. Because I am burning in the fire.'

"But Abraham said, 'Why should I send Lazarus to you in the fire? In the other world, whatever you wanted, you got. But Lazarus saw only sorrow, so now he must rejoice. And of course he would want to do this, but it is impossible because there is a big pit between us and you, and it is impossible to get around it. We are the living, but you are the dead.'

"Then the rich man said, 'Well, then, Lord Abraham, at least send scab-covered Lazarus to my home, please. I have five brothers and I feel sorry for them. Let him tell them everything and show them the dangers of wealth. Otherwise they may fall into this same torment.'

"But Abraham said, 'They already know that it is dangerous. Moses and all of the prophets have also told them this.'

"And the rich man said, 'Everything would be better if someone from among the dead was resurrected and went to them, they would repent more fully.'

"But Abraham said, 'If they do not listen to Moses and the prophets, they will still not listen, even if the dead are resurrected.'

"All people know that one must share with his brother and do good to people. But the entire law of Moses and the writings of all the prophets speak exclusively about this very thing. You know this, but you cannot do it because you love wealth."

And a wealthy leader of the orthodox came to Jesus and said to him, "You good and blessed teacher, what should I do to receive eternal life?"

Jesus said, "Why do you call me good? Only the father is good. But if you want to have life, then keep the commandments."

And the leader said, "There are many commandments. Which ones, specifically?" And Jesus said, "Do not kill, do not be promiscuous, do not steal, do not lie, also honor your father, do his will and love your neighbor as yourself."

And the orthodox leader said, "I have been keeping all of these commandments since childhood, but I am asking what else I must do, according to your teaching."

Jesus looked at him, at his clothing, smiled and said, "There is one little thing you have not done, you have not actually fulfilled what you said you had. If you want to keep these commandments—do not kill, do not be promiscuous, do not steal, do not lie, and the main commandment love your neighbor as yourself—then go, right now, and sell all your property and give the money to the poor. Then you will be doing your father's will."

The leader heard this, frowned, and walked away, because he did not want to part with his property.

And Jesus said to his students, "Now you see that there is no way to be rich and to fulfill your father's will."

The students were horrified at these words. But Jesus repeated them again and said, "Yes, children, it is impossible for him who holds his own property to be within the father's will. A camel will sooner make it through the eye of a needle than the man who relies on his riches will perform the father's will."

And they were even more horrified and said, "But what happens next? Doing this would make it impossible to keep yourself alive."

But he said, "To man it seems that it is impossible to keep oneself alive without possessions, but God can save man's life without possessions."

Once Jesus was walking through the city of Jericho. And in this city lived the chief of the tax collectors, a rich man, and his name was Zacchaeus. This Zacchaeus had heard of Jesus's teaching and had come to believe in it. And when he discovered that Jesus was in Jericho, he wanted to see him. There was such a large crowd around that it was impossible to get close to him. And Zacchaeus was not very tall. So then he ran ahead and climbed into a tree in order to see Jesus as he walked past the tree.

And Jesus saw him in this position as he walked past, and realized that the man believed in his teaching, so he said, "Climb down from the tree and go home, I will come to you."

Zacchaeus climbed down, ran home, prepared for the meeting with Jesus, and received him joyfully.

And the people began to judge Jesus and say about him, "Now he has gone to the home of the tax collector, a crook."

And at that time Zacchaeus said to Jesus, "Look, Lord, at what I am doing. I am giving half of my property to the poor, and from the rest I will repay my debt four times over to those that I have offended."

And Jesus said, "And you have been saved by these acts. You were dead, but now you are alive. You had gotten lost but now you have been found, because in your actions, like Abraham, when he intended to stab his own son, you have shown your faith. Because this is what man's entire life amounts to: seeking out and saving the thing that is perishing within one's soul. A sacrifice cannot be measured by its size."

It happened once that Jesus and his students were sitting opposite a poor box. People offered all their possessions into the box for God. Wealthy people as well came up to the box and put large amounts in. But one impoverished widow came up to it and deposited two mites.

And Jesus pointed toward her and said to his students, "Now, you see that this widow, a poor woman, deposited two mites; she has deposited more than all the others."

It happened once that Jesus was in the home of Simon the Leper. And a woman entered the home. And this woman had a jar of expensive, fine oil worth three hundred rubles. Jesus told his students that his death was near. The woman heard this and felt reluctant to part with him and wanted to demonstrate her love and anoint his head with oil. And she forgot all about how much the oil cost and broke open the jar and anointed his head and feet, spilling the remaining oil. And the students began to discuss among themselves what an evil deed she had done.

Judas, the one that would later betray Jesus, said, "Look how much potential good has been lost in vain! One could have sold that oil for three hundred rubles and clothed so many poor people!" And the students began to scold the woman, who then became embarrassed and did not know whether she had done a good or bad thing.

Then Jesus said to them, "You are embarrassing the woman for nothing. She truly did good, so you are referring to the poor in vain. If you want to do good to the poor, then do it. They will always be available. Why talk about them now? If you feel bad for the poor, go and have mercy on them, do good to them; but this woman had mercy on me and did some actual good because she gave away what she had. Which one of you can know what is needed and what is not needed? How do you know that anointing my head with oil is a superfluous act? She poured her oil on me as if to prepare my body for burial, that is why her act was necessary. She truly fulfilled the father's will, she forgot herself and had mercy on another. She forgot about accounting in terms of mortal life and gave away all that she had."

And Jesus said, "My teaching is to fulfill the will of the father, but one can only fulfill the will of the father with actions, and not with words. If any son responds to his father's commands by saying 'I will, I will,' but does nothing that the father has required, then obviously he is not fulfilling the father's will.

"But if the other son so much as says, 'I do not want to obey,' but then goes and fulfills his father's commands, then he is, after all, fulfilling the father's will. With people, it is just the same. The one who speaks out and says 'I am within the father's will' is really not. No, the one who does what the father wants is within his will."

Chapter Seven

THE FATHER AND I ARE ONE

The true food of everlasting life is the fulfillment of the
father's will and communion with him.

GIVE US OUR DAILY BREAD

*In answer to the Jews' demands for proof, Jesus says, "The truth of my
teaching can be proven by the fact that I teach not from myself but from our
common father. I teach what is good for the father of all people and therefore what is good for all people.*

*"Do what I say, keep the five commandments, and you will see that
what I say is true. Keeping these five commandments will drive out all evil
from the world and this will verify their truthfulness. The law of Moses
teaches the fulfillment of people's will, therefore it is full of contradictions;
my teaching teaches us to fulfill the father's will and therefore it leads all
things toward unity."*

*The Jews do not understand him and seek external evidences regard-
ing whether or not he is the prophesied Christ. In response to this, he tells
them, "Do not try and ascertain who I am and whether or not I am written of in your prophecies, but ponder my teaching concerning our common
father. You do not have to believe in me as a person, just believe in the words
that I speak in the name of the common father of all people. There can be
no proofs of my teaching. It is light. And just as it is impossible to shine a
light onto light itself, it is impossible to prove the truthfulness of truth. My
teaching is light, and whoever is in the darkness should move toward it."*

But the Jews ask him again who he is, in terms of the flesh. He tells them, "I am what I have said to you from the beginning: a man, the son of the father of life. Only he who understands the same of himself will cease to be a slave and will become free. Just as how a slave will not always remain in his master's household, but a son remains forever, likewise a person living as a slave to the flesh will not always remain in life, but a person who fulfills the father's will through the spirit will always remain in life.

"In order to understand me, you should understand that my father is not like your father, the one that you call God. Your father is a God of the flesh, but my father is the spirit of life. Your father is a God of vengeance and a murderer of men, one who punishes people; whereas my father gives life. Therefore we are children of different fathers. I seek truth and you want to kill me for it, in order to appease your God. Whoever believes in my teaching will not see death."

The Jews say, "How can a person not die if even the people who pleased God most, like Abraham, died? How can you say that you and those that believe in your teaching will not die?"

Jesus answered this by saying, "I am speaking of that same source of life which you call God and which is within people, I say that it has been, it is, and it will be, and that death does not exist for it. Any demands for proof of the truthfulness of my teaching are similar to people demanding evidence from a blind man on how and why he came to see the light.

"A healed blind man, remaining the same person that he was before, could only say that he was blind, but now he sees. Exactly this and nothing more can be said by the person who did not previously understand the meaning of life, but then suddenly came to comprehend it. Such a person would only say that he previously did not know true goodness in life, but now he knows it. Like the healed blind man, who says 'I do not know anything about the correctness of the healing or the sinfulness of the healer, nor anything about some different, better healing. I know only one thing and that is that I was blind, but now I see,' he cannot say anything about whether it is a correct teaching, whether the one who revealed it to him is a sinner, or whether there is some other, better goodness to be known. He will just say, 'Before I did not see the meaning of life, but now I see it and I do not know anything more than this.'

"People will devote themselves to my teaching because it alone promises life to all. Just as the sheep follow their shepherd who gives them food and life, people accept my teaching because it gives life to all. And just as the sheep do not follow after the thieves that climb into the fold but scatter in every direction, people cannot believe in teachings of violence and punishment. The only good shepherds are the ones that are their own masters and love the sheep and give their lives for them, whereas the bad ones are hired workers that do not love the sheep. Teachers are the same; the only true teacher is the one who does not care for himself. My teaching is to not care for yourself but to give up your mortal life for the life of the spirit. I teach that, and I do it as well."

The Jews still do not understand him and continue to seek external proofs as to whether or not he is the Christ and therefore whether or not to believe him. Jesus says to them, "You should believe in actions, not words. By the actions that I tell you to perform, you can understand whether or not I teach the truth. Do as I do, and do not get caught up in figuring out the words. I am the son of man—the same as the father. I am not the Christ, I am greater than Christ. I am the same as what you call God and what I call the father. And in your own scriptures it is said that God told people, 'You are gods.' In his spirit, every man is the son of the father. If he fulfills the father's will, then he communes with the father. If I fulfill his will, then the father is within me and I am within the father."

Jesus asks his students how they understand his teaching about the son of man. Simon Peter answers him, "Your teaching is based on the fact that you are the son of the God of life and that God is the life of the spirit residing within a person."

And Jesus says to him, "This is not just true of me, but of all people. True life rests on this concept. For this life, there is no death."

After this the Jews attempted to condemn Jesus to death, and Jesus went to Galilee to stay with his family. The Jewish holiday for the renewal of the tabernacle had arrived and Jesus's brothers gathered to go to a celebration and they called Jesus to go with them.

They did not believe in his teaching and they said to him, "Now, you say that the Jewish way of worshipping God is incorrect, but that you know that the real way to worship God is with actions. If you really think that no one but you knows the true way to worship God, then come with us to the celebration. There will be lots of people, so you can then announce in front of everyone that the teachings of Moses are false. If everyone believes you, then your students will all see that you are correct. Otherwise, why hide? You say that our worship of God is false, that you know the true way to worship. If that is the case, you should demonstrate it for everyone."

And Jesus said to them, "For you there is a special time and place to worship God, but for me there is no special time to worship God. I am working for God always and everywhere. And I demonstrate that very thing to people. I show them that their worship of God is false, and for that, they hate me.

"You go to the celebration and I will go when I feel like it."

And his brothers left, but he stayed behind and only went later, arriving in the middle of the celebration. The Jews were bothered that he did not respect their holiday and did not attend it. And many argued about his teaching. Some said that he spoke the truth, and others said that he was just confusing the people.

In the middle of the celebration, Jesus entered the temple and began to teach the people that their worship of God was false, that God was not to be worshipped in temples and with offerings, but in spirit and in action, by keeping the five commandments. Everyone listened to him and they were amazed that he was versed in such wisdom, despite having no training.

And Jesus, having heard that they were amazed by his wisdom, said to them, "My teaching is not my own, but his who sent me. If anyone wants to fulfill the will of that spirit that sent us into life, he will realize that I did not invent this, but that it is teaching from God. Because he who invents things from his own thoughts seeks out what is in his own mind, but he that seeks what is in the mind of the one who sent him is just. There is no falseness in him.

"Your law of Moses is not the law of the father and because of that, those who follow it are not keeping the father's law, they are committing evil and lies. I teach you only to fulfill the father's will and in my teaching there can be no contradictions. But your written law of Moses is completely full of contradictions. Do not base your judgments on the exterior, but base your judgments on the spirit."

And many said, "But they just told us that he is a false prophet. And here he is, criticizing the law, and no one is saying anything to him. Maybe he actually is a true prophet, maybe the leaders have recognized him. There is only one thing that we cannot believe about him, because it is said that when God's messenger comes, no one will know where he is from. But we know where he is from by birth, and we know all of his relatives."

The people still did not understand his teaching and they still sought proof.

Then Jesus said to them, "You know me and where I am from according to the flesh, but you do not know where I am from according to the spirit. The one whom I come from, according to the spirit, is the only one you should know, but you do not know him. If I said that I am the Christ, you would be believing in me as a man, and not in the father, who is within me and within you. And the father is the only one you should believe in.

"I am not here among you for a long period of my life. I show you the path to that source of life from which I emerged. Yet you asked for evidence from me and you want to condemn me. If you do not know this path now, then when I am no longer here you will not be able to find it. You should not be condemning me, you should be following me.

"Whoever does what I teach will find out whether what I'm telling you is true. The one for whom mortal life has not become food for the spirit does not seek truth, like the thirsty man seeking water, and such a person cannot understand me. The one who thirsts for truth, let him come to me and drink. He who believes in my teaching will receive true life. He will receive the life of the spirit."

And many came to believe in his teaching and said, "What he says is true and it comes from God."

Others did not understand him and still sought in the prophecies to find evidence that he was from God. And many argued with him, but no one could challenge him. The educated orthodox sent their assistants to contend with him.

But their assistants returned to the orthodox bishops and said, "We cannot get anywhere with him."

And the bishops said, "Why did you not confound him?"

And they answered, "No man has ever spoken like he does."

Then the orthodox said, "The fact that he cannot be challenged and that the people all believe his teaching means nothing. We do not believe and none of the leaders believe. But these damned people have always been stupid and untrained; they believe anyone."

And Nicodemus, the one to whom Jesus has explained his teaching, said to the bishops, "You cannot condemn the man without having listened to him and without having understood what he is trying to accomplish."

And they said to him, "There is nothing to judge or listen to. We know that no prophet could possibly come from Galilee."

At another time, Jesus spoke with the orthodox and said to them, "There can be no proofs of the truthfulness of my teaching, just as light cannot be shined on light. My teaching is the true light that people can see by and that demonstrates what is good and what is bad. Therefore it is impossible to prove my teaching. It proves everything else. Whoever follows me will not be in the darkness but will have life. Life and light are one and the same."

But the orthodox said, "You are the only one that says so."

And he answered them, "If I am the only one that says so, then all the same it is my truth because I know where I came from and where I am going. According to my teaching there is a meaning of life, according to yours there is not. Besides, I do not teach this alone, but my father, the spirit, teaches the same."

They said, "Where is your father?"

He said, "You do not understand my teaching, so you do not know my father. You do not know where you are from and where you are going. I am guiding you, but instead of following me, you are trying to ascertain who I am, therefore you cannot come to that salvation and life toward which I am guiding you. And you will perish if you remain in this delusion and do not follow after me."

And the Jews asked, "Who are you?"

He said, "From the very beginning, I have said: I am the son of man, recognizing the spirit as my father; and I tell the world what I have understood from the father. And when you glorify the son of man, then you will find out what I am because I act and speak not for myself as a man. All that I say and all that I teach are just what the father has taught me. And he who sent me is always with me, and the father will not abandon me because I do his will.

"Whoever holds to my knowledge, whoever fulfills the will of the father, will be truly taught by me. In order to know truth, one must do good to people. Whoever does evil to people loves darkness and moves toward that; whoever does good to people moves toward light. And therefore, in order to understand my teaching, one must perform acts of goodness. Whoever does good will come to know truth; he will be free from evil and death. Because everyone who is deceived becomes a slave to their own delusion.

"But just as the slave does not live in the master's house indefinitely, whereas the master's son always remains in the household, likewise a man, if he has become deceived in life and becomes a slave to his delusions, will not live indefinitely, but will die. Only the one who is in the truth will remain living indefinitely. The truth is to be found not in being a slave, but in being a son. And so, if you are deceived, you will be slaves and will die. But if you are in the truth, then you will be free sons, and you will live.

"You say to yourselves that you are the sons of Abraham, that you know the truth. But here, you want to kill me because you do not understand my teaching. So it turns out that I speak what I have understood from my father and you want to do what you have understood from your father."

They said, "Our father is Abraham."

Jesus said to them, "If you were the sons of Abraham, you would perform the same actions he performed. But here, you want to kill me because I told you what I have understood from God. Abraham did not do that. So it would seem that you aren't serving God, but you are serving some other father of yours."

They said to him, "We are not bastards, we are all children of one father, we are all God's."

And Jesus said to them, "If your father were the same as mine, then you would love me, because I come from the father. After all, I did not give birth to myself. You are not children of the same father as I am, and because of that you do not understand my words, my knowledge finds no place within you. If I come from the father, and you come from that same father, then you could not desire to kill me. If you desire to kill me, then we are not from the same father.

"I am from the father of goodness, from God, and you are from the devil, from the father of evil. You desire the lusts of your father the devil; he has always been a murderer and a liar, and there is no truth within him. If he says anything, the devil, then he says his own personal thing, and not something that would be common to all, so he is the father of lies. Therefore, you are servants of the devil and are his sons.

"There, you can see how simple it is to expose your delusion. If I am deceived, then expose me. But if there is no delusion in me, then why not believe me?"

And the Jews began to curse him and said that he was mad.

He said, "I am not mad, I just honor the father and you want to kill me for it. So it seems that you are not my brothers, but are children of some other father. I am not the one to confirm my correctness, it is the truth that speaks for me. And therefore I will repeat to you: whoever comprehends my teaching and lives by it will not see death."

And the Jews said, "Is it really wrong for us to call you a mad Samaritan? You have exposed yourself. The prophets died, Abraham died, but you say that whoever lives by your teaching will not see death. Abraham died, but you won't die? What, are you greater than Abraham?"

The Jews were still puzzling over the fact that he was Jesus from Galilee, and the question of whether or not he was an important prophet, so they forgot all that he had told them, that he had said nothing about himself as a person, but that he spoke only of the spirit that was within him.

And Jesus said, "I do not do anything myself. If I had been talking about myself, about how things seem to me, then everything I said would have meant nothing, but what I have been speaking of is the source of all things, which you call God. And you did not and do not know the actual God, but I know him. I cannot say that I do not know him. I would be a liar, just like you, if I said that I do not know him. I know him, I know his will and I fulfill it. Abraham, your father, saw and rejoiced in my knowledge."

The Jews said, "You are fifty years old,* how could you have lived at the same time as Abraham?"

He said, "Before Abraham existed, the knowledge of goodness existed, this is what I have been telling you about."

The Jews picked up stones to beat him, but he left them.

And along the road, Jesus saw a man that had been blind from birth.

And his students asked, "Who is to blame that this man is blind from birth. Is it his fault or his parents', since they did not educate him?"

And Jesus answered, "Neither he nor his parents are to blame, but this is how God operates, creating light where there had been darkness. Wherever my teaching goes, it becomes the light of the world."

And Jesus revealed his teaching of being the son of God the spirit to the blind man, and when the blind man experienced the teaching, he experienced light. And those that previously knew this man could not recognize him. He was similar to how he had been before, but had now become a different person.

He said, "I am the same, but Jesus revealed to me that I am the son of God, and light opened up to me and I saw what I had never seen before."

This man was called before the orthodox teachers, and it was the Sabbath. And the orthodox asked him how he had begun to understand all things, when previously he had been blind.

He said, "I do not know how, I just know that now I understand everything."

They said, "You do not understand this in a godly way because

---

* Most translations present this statement as something close to "You are not yet fifty . . ." For some reason Tolstoy decides to make it a precise statement of age.

Jesus did this on the Sabbath; moreover, a worldly man cannot enlighten people."

And they began to argue.

And then they asked the enlightened man, "What do you think of him?"

He said, "I think he is a prophet."

The Jews could not believe that he had previously been blind, but that now he could see light, so they had called his parents and asked them, "Is this your son, the one who was blind from birth? How is it that he is now enlightened?"

The parents said, "We know that this is our son and that he has been blind since birth. But how it happened that he is now enlightened, we do not know. He is an adult, ask him."

The orthodox called the man a second time and said, "Pray to our true God, because we know for certain that that man who enlightened you is a worldly man and is not from God."

And the enlightened one said, "As to the question of whether the man is from God or not, I do not know. I know only one thing: that I did not see the light before and now I see it."

And the orthodox asked again, "What did he do with you, how did he enlighten you?"

He said, "I already told you, but you do not believe me. If you want to be his students, then I will tell you again."

And they began to curse him and said, "You may be his student, but we are students of Moses. God himself spoke with Moses. But we do not even know where this one comes from."

And the man answered and said, "It is amazing that he has enlightened me, but you still don't know where he comes from. God does not listen to sinners, he listens to those that honor him and do his will. It could never be that a man who is not from God could enlighten a blind man. If he were not from God, he could not do anything."

And the orthodox became angry and said, "You are completely immersed in delusion, and yet you want to teach us."

So they threw him out.

And Jesus said, "My teaching is an awakening of life. Whoever believes in my teaching, despite dying mortally, will remain living, and everyone who lives and believes in me will not die."

And again, for the third time, Jesus taught the people.

He said, "People are devoting themselves to my teaching, and not because I prove it myself. It is impossible to prove the truth. Truth proves everything else. But people devote themselves to my teaching because it is unified and is familiar to people, and it promises life. For the people, my teaching is like the familiar voice of the shepherd is for the sheep, when he comes in at the gate and gathers them in order to take them to pasture. No one believes your teaching because it is foreign to people, and people notice within it your lusts. For the people, your teaching is the same as the appearance of a stranger who does not enter at the gate, but climbs over the fence for the sheep. The sheep do not know him and can sense that he is an outlaw.

"My teaching is the one truth, like the one gate for the sheep. All of your teaching from the law of Moses is a lie. It is all like thieves and outlaws for the sheep. Whoever devotes themselves to my teaching will find true life, just as the sheep will go out and find food if they follow the shepherd. Because a thief only comes intending to steal, plunder and destroy, but the shepherd comes to give life. And only my teaching promises and gives true life.

"There are those shepherds for whom the sheep are their entire lives and who would give those lives for the sheep. These are true shepherds. But there are also hired workers, those that are not too troubled about the sheep, because they are just hired workers and the sheep do not belong to them, those who, if a wolf comes near, drop everything and run, allowing the wolf to destroy the sheep. These are not true shepherds.

"Likewise, there are false teachers, those that have no stake in the lives of people, and there are true ones, those that give their souls for the lives of the people. I am such a teacher. My teaching is to give my life for the people. No one can take it from me, I myself am freely giving it for the people, in order to receive true life. I received this commandment from my father. And just as the father knows me, I know the father, and therefore I lay down my life for the people. And for that, the father loves me, because I am keeping his commandments. And all people, not only those here and now, but all people will understand my voice and they will all gather together as one; all people will be unified and their teaching will be one."

And the Jews surrounded him and said, "Everything that you say is difficult to understand, and it does not correspond with scripture. Do not torment us, just tell us, simply and directly: are you that Messiah who is supposed to come into the world, according to our scripture?"

And Jesus answered them, "I already told you who I am, but you do not believe me. If you do not believe my words, then believe my actions. Through them, you will understand who I am and for what purpose I have come. But you do not believe, because you do not follow me. Whoever follows after me and does what I say will understand me. And whoever understands my teaching and fulfills it will receive actual life.

"My father has united them with me and no one can divide us. The father and I are one."

And the Jews were offended by this and picked up stones to beat him.

But he said to them, "I have shown you many good works, revealing to you teachings about my father; for which of these good works do you want to beat me?"

They said, "It is not for goodness that we want to beat you, but because you, a man, are making yourself God."

And Jesus answered them, "Well, this very claim is made in your own scripture, after all. It is said that God himself told the evil rulers, 'You are gods.' If he called even the unholy ones Gods, then why do you consider it sacrilege to refer to something that God lovingly sent into the world as the son of God? Every person is a son of God in spirit. If I do not live in a godly way, then do not believe that I am a son of God. If, however, I do live in a godly way, then believe, based on my life, that I am from the father and then you will understand that the father is within me and I am within him."

And Jesus said, "My teaching is an awakening of life. Whoever believes in my teaching, although he may die in the flesh, will remain living and everyone who lives and believes in me will not die."

And the Jews began to argue. Some said that he was possessed.

Others said, "There's no way a possessed man can enlighten people."

The Jews did not know what to do with him, and they could not condemn him.

And he went again across the Jordan and remained there.

And many came to believe in his teaching and said that it was true, just as the teaching of John was true. And so, many people believed in his teaching.

Once, Jesus asked his students, "Tell me, how do people understand my teaching concerning the son of man?"

They said, "Some understand it like the teaching of John, others just like the prophecies of Isaiah, still others say that it resembles the teaching of Jeremiah; they understand that you are a prophet."

He said, "And what do you understand of my teaching?"

And Simon Peter said to him, "In my opinion, your teaching is that you are the chosen son of the God of life. You teach that God is the life that exists within man."

And Jesus said to him, "You are lucky, Simon, that you have understood that. A person could not have revealed that to you, but you understand it because the God within you has revealed it to you. It was not mortal reasoning, and it was not me with my words that revealed it to you, but God my father revealed it to you directly. And on that rests the foundation for the gathering of chosen people, for whom there is no death."

Chapter Eight

LIFE OUTSIDE OF TIME

And therefore only life in the present is true life.

THIS DAY

To the apostles' doubts regarding the sort of reward they would have for renouncing mortal life, Jesus answers:

For a man who has understood the teaching, there can be no rewards. First of all, because the man who leaves behind his loved ones and his belongings in the name of this teaching obtains one hundred times more loved ones and more belongings. Second of all, because a man who seeks rewards is pursuing a situation in which he has more than another person does, and this practice is especially repellent to the fulfillment of the father's will. For the kingdom of heaven there is no such thing as more or less: all are equal. Those who seek rewards for goodness are like workers who would demand more pay for themselves than for others paid by their master only because they consider themselves to be more worthy than others. Reward and punishment, debasement and exaltation, do not exist for someone who understands the teaching. No one can be higher or more important than someone else. Everyone can fulfill the fathers' will, but in doing so, not one person will make himself more senior or important or better than another. Only kings and those who serve them can think this way.

According to my teaching, there can be no elders, because he who wants to be better should become the slave of all. This is the essence of the teaching: man is given life not to be served, but to offer his whole life in service of other people.

In order to not think about rewards and exaltation for yourself, you must understand that the meaning of life is in the fulfillment of the father's will; that what the father has given away should return to him. Like a shepherd leaving the whole flock to go search for the one missing sheep and like the woman who tears apart everything to find the lost kopeck, likewise, the activity of the father manifests itself to us by pulling toward itself all that formerly belonged to it.

You must understand what true life is. True life always manifests itself in the phenomenon that what was lost returns to its place, that what has fallen into a sleep awakens. People who have true life return to their source; if they have true life, they are incapable of rating, as the custom is, who is better and who is worse, but as participants in the father's life, they can only rejoice at returning what was lost to the father. If a son falls from the path and wanders from the father but then repents and returns to the father, then can the other sons really be envious of the father's joy and refuse to rejoice at the brother's return?

In order to believe the teaching, in order to change your life and fulfill the teaching, external proofs are unnecessary. One does not need the promise of rewards, but a clear understanding of what true life is. If people think they can be all-powerful masters of life, that life is given to them for the lusts of the flesh, then it is obvious that every act of sacrifice for another will seem to them a deed worthy of a reward and without reward they will not do anything. If the share croppers, who forgot that they were given a garden on the condition that they give the fruit to the master, were required to make their payment without any reward, they would chase out the payment collector. And if he were to keep reminding them about the payment, they would kill him. That is how the people who call themselves the masters of life see things and they do not understand that life is a gift of knowledge which requires the fulfillment of its will. One must understand that man can do nothing on his own and that if he gives away his mortal life for the good, then there should be no thanks or reward expected. You must understand that, in doing good, a man does only what he is obligated to do, what he cannot leave unfulfilled. Only by understanding his life in that way can a man have enough belief to do true acts of goodness.

The kingdom of heaven, which I preach, is based on this understanding of life. This kingdom of heaven is invisible, it is not the sort of kingdom that exists somewhere and could be pointed to. It is made up of people's knowledge. The whole world has lived and still lives by old traditions: they eat, they drink, they work, they marry, they die and right alongside this, within people's souls, the kingdom of heaven lives. The kingdom of heaven is people's knowledge, like a tree in springtime, growing up out of itself.

The true life of fulfilling the father's will is not the life that has passed or the life that will be, but life right now. And therefore, you must never become weak for living. People are positioned to preserve life—not the past, not the future, but the life that they are presently living—and in it to fulfill the will of the father. If they exit this life, not having fulfilled the father's will, then they will not return. They are like the nightwatchman, positioned so as to watch through the entire night, who fails at his job if he falls asleep for even one minute, when a thief may approach. And therefore a man should bring all of his strength to the present hour, because only in that hour can he fulfill the father's will. Fulfilling the father's will is good for all people, since his will is the welfare of all. Only those who do good live.

Jesus said, "Whoever is not ready for all suffering and deprivation in the flesh has not understood me. Whoever labors for the best in mortal life destroys the true life. But whoever destroys his mortal life by doing my teaching will receive true life."

And at these words, Peter said to him, "We have obeyed you here, we have discarded all of our cares, all of our belongings, and have followed after you. What sort of reward will we have for this?"

Jesus said to him, "Everyone who has given up his home, sisters, brothers, father, mother, wife, children, and land for my teaching, receives one hundred times more sisters, brothers, land and anything that he needs, and apart from the things of this life, he receives life outside of time. There are no rewards in the kingdom of heaven. The kingdom of heaven itself is a goal and a reward. In the kingdom all are equal: there are no first, there are no last.

"Because the kingdom of heaven is like this: The master of the house went out in the morning to hire workers for the garden. He hired workers for one grivna a day and entered the garden and made them work.

"And again he went at lunchtime and hired some more and sent them to the garden to work and toward evening, he again hired more and sent them to work. And he agreed to pay each of them a grivna.

"It came time for payment and the master commanded for each to be paid the same. First, those who came last, and afterwards those who came first. And now, the first saw that the last were also being given a grivna. And they assumed that they would be given more than that; but the first were only given a grivna.

"And they took their money and said, 'What is this, they only worked one shift and we worked all four, how is it that we are being paid the same? It is unjust.'

"And the master came and said, 'What are you griping for, have I offended you somehow? I am paying you what I hired you for. Wasn't our agreement for a grivna? Take your money and go. But if I want to give the last the same thing that I gave you, do I not have the power to act on my own? Or is it that you saw how kind I am, and then became jealous?'

"In the kingdom of heaven there are no first and there are no last—it is the same for all."

Once, two of Jesus's students, Jacob and John, came to him and said, "Teacher! Promise that you will do for us what we ask."

He said, "What do you want?"

They said, "We want to be equal with you."

Jesus said to them, "You do not know what you are asking. You can live just as I do, you can purify yourself from mortal life just as I do, but to make you the same as me—that is not in my power. Every man must enter the father's will of his own power."

Having heard that, the other students became angry at the two brothers for wanting to be the same as the teacher, to be the most senior of the students.

Jesus called to them and said, "If you, brothers John and Jacob, asked me to make you the same as me in order to be the most senior of the students, then you have made a mistake. If, however, you, other students, are angry at them because these two wanted to have seniority over you, then you are mistaken also. In this world only kings and rulers count who is most senior, so that they can govern nations.

"But among you there can be no seniors and no juniors. Among you, in order to be greater than another, you must become a servant to all. Among you, whoever wants to be first must consider himself last. Because this is the will of the father concerning the son of man, that he live not to be served, but to serve all others himself and to give away his mortal life like a ransom for the life of the spirit."

And Jesus said to the people, "The father seeks to save the one that perishes. He rejoices in him just as the shepherd rejoices when he finds his one missing sheep. When one goes missing, he leaves behind the ninety-nine and goes to save the missing one. And if a peasant woman loses a kopeck, then of course she'll sweep out the whole hut and search until she has found it. The father loves his son and calls him to himself."

And he told them another parable about how it is impossible to elevate yourself by living in God's will.

He said, "If you are called to lunch, then you should not sit at the head of the table. It may happen that you will take the seat and someone more respected than you will arrive, and the master will say, 'Get out of there and leave it for he who is better than you.' Then you will be even more ashamed. It would be better for you to sit in the very last space instead. Then the master will find you and call you to a respected place. Then you will have honor. Likewise, in the kingdom of God there are no places of pride. Whoever elevates himself, in doing so will lower himself; and whoever lowers himself a bit, by doing so will elevate himself in the kingdom of God.

"There was a man who had two sons.

"The younger said to the father, 'Father! Give me my inheritance.' And the father gave it to him. The younger took his portion and went to a far-off place and wasted all of his holdings and became impoverished. And in that far-off place he wound up in a pigsty, and was so hungry that he ate the slop with the pigs.

"And he began to think of his living situation and said, 'Why did I separate and leave my father. Father had an abundance of everything. All of father's workers eat well. But here I am eating the same food as pigs. Let me go to my father, fall at his feet and say: I am guilty, father, before you and do not deserve to be your son. Take me on though, at the very least as a farmhand.'

"After thinking this, he went to his father. And when he was still just beginning to approach, his father instantly recognized him from far away and ran to meet him, embraced him and began to kiss him.

"And the son said, 'Father, I am guilty before you, I do not deserve to be your son.'

"But the father would not listen and said to the workers, 'Quickly, bring the very best clothes and the very finest boots, dress him and put boots on him. And run, catch the fatted calf and kill it, we are going to celebrate this: That my son was dead, but he has now returned to life, he had gotten lost, but now he has been found.'

"The older brother came in from the field and as he drew near, he heard that music was being played in the house. He called a serving boy and said, 'What sort of celebration is going on in there?'

"And the boy said, 'Have you really not heard? Your brother has returned and your father is rejoicing. He commanded us to kill the fatted calf to celebrate the return of his son.'

"The older brother was offended and did not go into the home. But the father came out and called him.

"And he said to his father, 'Father, how many years now have I worked for you, not missing a single command, and you've never slaughtered the fatted calf for me. But my younger brother left the home, and he gambled away all his estate with drunks, and yet you have now slaughtered the fatted calf for him.'

"And the father said, 'You are always with me, and everything that I have is yours. And you ought not to be offended, but to rejoice that your brother, who was among the dead, has returned to life; he was lost but he has now been found.'

"A master planted a garden, labored over it, arranged it, did everything so that the garden would produce as much fruit as possible. And he sent some workers into this garden, so that they would labor, gather fruit and, according to their agreement, pay him for use of the garden.

"The master is the father, the garden is the world, the workers are people. The father sent his son, the son of man, into the world so that people would give the father back the knowledge of life that he placed inside them.

"Time passed and the master sent one of his workers to collect the payment. The father had not ceased to tell the people that they were obligated to fulfill his will. The workers chased off the master's messenger empty-handed and they continued to live, imagining that the garden was their own, that they themselves occupied it by their own grace. People have chased off the reminder of the father's will and continue to live each for himself, imagining that they live for the joys of mortal life.

"Then the master sent to them again, this time sending some of his favorites and even his son to remind them about their debt. But the workers had become completely foolish and imagined to themselves that if they killed the master's son, who had come to remind them that the garden was not theirs, then they would finally be left in peace. And so they killed him.

"People do not love to be reminded that there is a spirit that lives within them and that it is eternal, but that they are not eternal; and so they killed, as much as they could, the consciousness of that spirit. They wrapped the grivna they had been given in a handkerchief and buried it in the ground.

"What could the master do? Nothing but drive out those workers and send in others. What can the father do? Keep planting until fruit is produced. And this very thing is what he does. People have not understood and still do not understand that this consciousness of the spirit within them, a consciousness they suppress since it inhibits them, is actually the essence of their lives. They discard the rock on which everything rests.

"And those who do not take the life of the spirit as a foundation will not enter into the kingdom of heaven and will not receive life. In order to have faith and receive life, one must understand one's condition, and not wait for a reward."

Then the students said to Jesus, "Multiply our faith within us; tell us something that will make us believe in the life of the spirit more strongly and not long for mortal life. Look how much we must give, we must give away everything for the life of the spirit. And you say yourself that there is no reward."

And at this, Jesus told them, "If you could have the same faith as your assurance that a giant tree will grow from a birch seed, if you could believe similarly that within you is the single embryo of the spirit, from which true life will develop, you would not need to ask me to multiply your faith within you. Faith does not consist of believing in something amazing, faith consists of understanding your own condition and understanding where you can turn for salvation. If you understand your own condition, then you won't wait for any rewards. You will believe in what has already been entrusted to you.

"When the master returns from the field with his worker, then of course he does not immediately sit his worker down to the table. But he commands him to gather the livestock and prepare him some dinner and only then does he say to the worker, 'Sit down, drink and eat.' The master does not think to thank the worker for doing what he was supposed to do. And the worker, if he understands that he is a worker, is not offended, but works, believing that he will receive what he deserves.

"Likewise, you should fulfill the will of the father and work from the premise that we are worthless workers, that we are only doing what we are obligated to do, and do not expect rewards, being satisfied that you receive what you deserve. You do not need to worry about this in order to have faith that there will be a reward and that there will be life; it cannot be otherwise. You must worry that you do not destroy this life and you must not forget that it was given to us so that we bear its fruits and fulfill the father's will.

"Therefore always be prepared, like servants waiting for the master, to immediately, as soon as he arrives, open the gate for him. The servants do not know when he is to return, whether it will be early or late, so they should always be prepared. And if they greet the master, then they have fulfilled his will, and that is good for them. The same is true in life. Always, in every minute of the present you must live the life of the spirit, not thinking about the past or the future and not saying to yourself, 'Only then or there will I do this or that.'

"If the master knew that a thief was coming, then he would not sleep. Likewise, you must never sleep, because the life of the son of man is without time, he lives only in the present and does not know when the beginning and the end of his life are.

"Our life is the same as the life of a slave whom the master has left in the position of seniority at his home. It is good for that slave if he always does the will of the master. But if he says, 'The master will not be coming soon,' and forgets to do the master's business, then the master will return by surprise and will throw him out.

"And so, do not despair, but always live by the spirit in the present. Time does not exist for the life of the spirit. Look after yourself so that you do not become bitter and do not grow dim with drunkenness, gluttony, or worries, so that you do not miss the time of salvation. The time of salvation, like a net, is cast over all people; it is always present. And therefore, above all else, live the life of the son of man.

"The kingdom of heaven is similar to this: Ten virgins with lamps went to meet the groom. Five were smart and five were stupid. The stupid ones took their lamps but did not take any oil. But the smart ones took their lamps and some oil in reserve. While they waited for the groom, they began to doze off.

"When the groom approached, the stupid ones saw that they had only a little oil remaining. And they went to look for a place to buy oil, but while they were out, the groom arrived. And the smart virgins, who had oil, entered with him and the doors closed behind them.

"The virgins had needed to go and meet the groom with their lamps, only for this purpose. But they forgot that it was not just important that the lamps burn but that they burned at the right time.

And in order for them to burn at the right time, they needed to be burning constantly. Life exists only to elevate the son of man, and the son of man is always present. He is outside of time, and therefore, when serving him, you must live outside of time, strictly in the present. Therefore, make your efforts in the present, in order to enter into the life of the spirit. If you do not make the effort, you will not enter. You will say, 'We said this and that,' but there will be no good deeds and there will be an incomplete life. Because the son of man, like the one spirit, appears for each person according to how he served him.

"All people can be divided according to how they serve the son of man. By their actions they can be divided into two groups, just as the sheep and goats are in the flocks. Some will remain living and others will perish. Those who serve the son of man are the ones that will receive what has belonged to them from the beginning of the world, the life that they preserved. They preserved this life by serving the son of man. They nourished the hungry, dressed the naked, took in the traveler, visited the imprisoned. They lived by the son of man, they sensed that he was one in all people and therefore they loved him. But those who did not live by the son of man did not serve him, did not understand that he was one in all people and therefore they did not unite with him, so they lost the life he gave them and perished."

Chapter Nine

TEMPTATIONS

The illusions of temporal life conceal from people
the true life of the present.

AND FORGIVE US OUR DEBTS, AS WE
FORGIVE OUR DEBTORS

Man is born with the knowledge that true life can be found in fulfilling the
father's will. Children live by this; his will is evident in their actions. In
order to understand Jesus's teaching, you must understand how children
live and become like them. Children would never break the five command-
ments if their elders did not lead them into temptation. Temptation is the
evil that people do for imagined benefit in temporal life. People ruin chil-
dren by leading them into the temptation of breaking the commandments,
like the man who ties a grinding stone around another's neck and throws
him in a river. If there were no temptations, the world would be happy.
Temptations ruin people and therefore you must sacrifice everything in
order to keep from falling into temptation.

The temptation against the first commandment occurs when people
consider themselves pure before others, while considering others indebted
to them. To not fall into this temptation, people should remember that they
all carry an endless debt to the father and that they can only wash them-
selves of this debt by forgiving their brothers. Therefore people should for-
give their offenders, not being daunted if the offender continues to offend
again and again. No matter how many times a man may be offended, he
should forgive, not noting the evil, because the kingdom of heaven can only

be possible with forgiveness. If we do not forgive, then we are the same as the debtor who begs mercy of his master, is forgiven, but then continues to pressure those who owe him money. So what are we doing if we ourselves do not forgive? We do what we are afraid will be done to us. The father's will is goodness and evil is what distances us from the father. So why would we not try to extinguish this evil as quickly as possible if it can destroy us and deprive us of life? Evil binds us up in the ruins of the flesh, so we must diffuse it to obtain life.

The temptation against the second commandment occurs when we assume that woman has been created for the lusts of the flesh and that if we abandon one wife and take another we will have greater pleasure. To not fall into this temptation, you must remember that the father's will is not for man to find comfort in woman's beauty, but for everyone who has selected a wife to unite with her as one body. The father's will is that every husband have a wife and every wife have a husband. But when one replaces his wife, he deprives the wife of her husband and challenges another husband to leave his and take the abandoned one. You can choose not to have a wife, but having more than one wife is not possible since when you take a second wife, you break the father's will.

The temptation against the third commandment occurs when people establish systems of power for gain in temporal life and demand oaths from people. To not fall into this temptation people should remember that they are not obligated before anyone except God, and that this obligation is for their lives. People should look at the demands of power as if it were violence and, as in the commandment about not opposing evil, give away what the powers demand: their belongings and labor. But no one can bind you to actions in the future with promises and oaths. The oaths that they squeeze out of people turn them bad. A man who acknowledges life in the will of the father cannot promise his future actions because for every person there is nothing more holy than life.

The temptation against the fourth commandment occurs when people, giving into malice and vengeance, think that they can improve other people by doing so. If a man offends another, then people think that he must be punished and think that it is right to judge others. To not fall into this temptation, you must remember that people have not been called to judge, but to save one another, and that people cannot judge the wrongdoing of others, because they themselves are full of wrongdoing. The only way they can teach others is with their example of purity, forgiveness and love.

The temptation against the fifth commandment occurs when people presume a distinction between their own people and people of other nations and believe that it is necessary to protect themselves from other nations and to harm them. To not fall into this temptation, you must understand that all commandments can be combined into one: fulfill the will of the father, who has given life and goodness to all people, and do good to all people without making any distinctions. Other people may still make these distinctions between nations, and may go to war, but the man who fulfills the father's will does good to every person, no matter what nation he is from.

To avoid falling into any of these human errors, a man should think not of the flesh, but of the spirit. If a man has understood that life is only for the purpose of being within the will of the father at every present moment, then neither deprivation, nor suffering, nor death can frighten him.

Eternal life should not be understood as something that will be similar to our current life, happening in some place and at some point in time. True life in the will of the father has neither place nor time. It is impossible to imagine true life in terms of time or people. Those who have penetrated into true life live for the father. Even if for us they have died, for God, they are living. And therefore one commandment contains all else within it: love the source of life with all your strength, and by extension love every person who carries that source within them.

This source of life is the Christ for whom you are waiting. Anything that hides this source of life from people should be considered temptation. There is the temptation of the scribes and the old believers—do not give into it; there are the temptations of kingly power—do not give into

them; and there is also the most vicious temptation—that of the teachers
of faith who call themselves orthodox. Beware this temptation more than
the others because they, these self-proclaimed teachers, having thought up
false methods of worship, deceive you away from the true God. Instead of
serving the father of life with their actions, they have vaunted the word
and teach words, but the father doesn't need words, he needs actions. They
are occupied solely with the exterior, with the appearance of faith. Their
temptation is the root of all temptations because they have reviled what is
holy in the world and under the guise of goodness, they promote evil. You
know that no one can make himself a teacher of others. For all people there
is but one teacher—the lord of life, knowledge.

Once, some children were brought to Jesus, but his students began to push the children away.

Jesus saw that the students were pushing the children away, and he grew angry and said, "You are driving these children away pointlessly. Children are the best people because they all live in the will of the father. They are the ones whose place in the kingdom of heaven is secure. You should not drive them away, you should learn from them, because in order to live in the father's will, you must live as children live. Children always keep the five commandments that I have given you: children do not curse, they do not hold grudges against people, children do not whore, children do not take oaths for any reason, children do not oppose evil, they do not judge anyone, children do not see any distinctions between their own people and foreign ones, and therefore they are better than adults and are in the kingdom of heaven.

"If you do not renounce all of these temptations of the flesh and do not become like little children then you will not find yourself in the kingdom of heaven. Only he who understands that children are better than us, since they do not break the father's will, only he can understand my teaching. And whoever understands my teaching is simply comprehending the father's will.

"We cannot despise children because they are better than us and their souls are clean before the father. They are always with him. And not one child perishes due to the father's will. All children who perish do so only because of other people, because people deceive them away from the truth. Therefore we need to protect them and not tempt them away from their father and from true life. And the man who deceives them away from purity is committing evil. To deceive a child away from goodness, to tempt him with anger, lust, oaths, judgment, war is as bad as hanging a grinding stone around such a child's neck and throwing him into the water. It is difficult for him to swim to shore, and he will likely drown. It is just as difficult for a child to escape the temptation into which an adult has led him.

"People are unhappy in this world only because of temptations. Temptations are everywhere throughout the world. They always have been and always will be, and man will perish from temptations. So give all that you have, sacrifice everything, just do not fall into temptation. A fox may fall into a trap, but it will wriggle its paw out and run away, its paw will return to full health and the fox will remain living. You must do the same. Give away all that you have, just do not become entangled in temptation."

Beware the temptation against the first commandment: do not bear evil toward other people because they have offended you and you want to take vengeance on them.

"If a man offends you, remember that he is a son of the same father and that he is your brother. If he offended you, go and appeal to his conscience, face to face. If he listens to you, then you are both better off: you will have a new brother. If he doesn't listen, then call two or three others to be with you so that they can help convince him. And if he repents, forgive him. But if he continues to offend you, even seven times, but then seven times says, 'Forgive me,' then forgive him. If he does not listen, then tell a group of people who believe in my teaching. If that group of people also doesn't listen, then forgive him and have nothing more to do with him.

"Because the kingdom of God can be compared to the following: A king had begun to work out his accounts with his taxpayers. And they brought him one taxpayer who owed him one million rubles. And he had nothing to pay with. And the king would have had to confiscate his entire estate, his wife, his children, and the man himself. But the taxpayer began to beg for mercy from the king. And the king took mercy on him and forgave him his debt.

"And now that very taxpayer went home and came across another man. This man owed him fifty kopecks. The king's taxpayer caught the man and began to choke him, saying, 'Give me what you owe me.'

"And the man fell to his feet and said, 'Have patience with me, I will pay you in full.'

"But the taxpayer had no mercy and locked the man up, making him sit in prison until he could pay in full. Some other men saw this and went to the king, reporting what the taxpayer had done.

"Then the king called the taxpayer to him and said to him, 'I forgave you your entire tax, you evil dog, because you begged mercy of me. And so you ought to have mercy on your debtor because I took mercy on you.'

"And the king was overcome with anger and sent the taxpayer to be tortured until he could pay off his tax.

"The father will do the same with you if you do not forgive, with your whole heart, those who are guilty before you. You know, after all, that if a dispute is drawn out with a fellow man, that it is better to make peace with him instead of going to court. You know this and you do it because you know that if you go to court it will cost you more. The same is true with every type of malice. If you know that malice and evildoing distances you from the father, then unravel yourself from this malice as quickly as possible and make peace. After all, you know yourself that however you get yourself entangled on earth, you will be entangled the same way before the father. And however you disentangle yourself on earth, you will be similarly disentangled before the father.

"You must understand that if two or three are united on earth by my teaching, then they are already in possession of everything that they could desire from their father. Because where two or three are united in the name of the spirit that resides in man, then the spirit of man lives within them."

Beware the temptation against the second commandment, concerning how people exchange wives.

Once, Jesus was approached by the orthodox teachers who, testing him, said: "May a man abandon his wife?"

He said to them, "From the very beginning man has been created male and female, that is the will of the father. And for that reason a man will abandon his father and mother and cling to a wife. The husband and wife merge into one body. And so, for a man, his wife is the same as his own flesh. Therefore man should not break the natural law of God and divide what has been united.

"According to your law of Moses, it is said that a man can leave his wife and take another, but this is not true. By the father's will it is not so. I say to you that whoever abandons his wife is forcing her into debauchery as well as whoever may then associate with her. And, by leaving his wife, he spreads debauchery in the world."

And Jesus's students said to him, "It is too difficult to stay with one woman forever. If that is what is required then it would be better to not be married at all."

He said to them, "You can choose not to be married, but you

must understand what that means. If someone wants to live without taking a wife, then he must be completely clean and not have contact with women. Such people that have no contact with women certainly exist, but whoever loves women should unite with one wife, not abandon her and not look at any other women."

Beware the temptation against the third commandment, concerning how people force others to fulfill obligations and take oaths.

Once the tax collectors came to Peter and asked him, "What then, does your teacher not pay taxes?"

Peter said, "No, he does not pay," and he went and told Jesus that they had stopped him, and told him that everyone is required to pay taxes.

Then Jesus said to him, "The king doesn't collect taxes from his own sons, after all, and other than the king no one requires payments. Right? It is just the same with us. If we are the sons of God, then we are not obligated to anyone other than God and we are free from all other possible obligations. But if you are required to pay taxes, then pay them, and not because you are obligated to, but because you must not oppose evil. If not, then opposing evil will produce even greater evil."

Another time, the orthodox got together with the royal officials and they went to Jesus in order to catch him in his words.

They said to him, "You teach everything correctly. Tell us, are we obligated to pay a tax to the king or not?"

Jesus understood that they wanted to condemn him for not acknowledging obligation to the king.

He said to them, "Show me what you use to pay your tax to the king."

They gave him a coin.

He looked at the coin and said, "What is this here? Whose face is this and whose inscription?"

They said, "The king's."

And he said, "Well then give the king what is his, and do not give your soul, which is God's, to anyone except to God. Money, possessions, your labor, offer it to whoever demands it of you, but do not give your soul to anyone but God. Your orthodox teachers travel everywhere and force people to take oaths and promise that they will keep the law. But in doing this they are only perverting people and making them worse than whatever they may have been before. It is impossible to covenant your body for your soul. God is within your soul, so it is impossible to promise God to other people."

Beware the temptation against the fourth commandment, concerning how people judge and punish other people and call others to participate in these judgments and punishments.

Once, Jesus's students came to a village and asked to be given a place to sleep, but they were not admitted.

Then the students went to Jesus and complained about this, saying, "We wish they would be struck dead by lightning for this."

Jesus said, "You still have no understanding of who you are in spirit. I am not teaching you how to destroy people, but how to save them."

Once, a man came to Jesus and said, "Command my brother to give me the inheritance."

Jesus said to him, "No one has made me a judge for you, and I will not judge anyone. And you cannot judge anyone."

Once, the orthodox brought a woman to Jesus and said:

"Look at this woman who was caught in prostitution. According to the law we are to beat her with rocks. What do you say?"

Jesus did not answer them, but waited for them to change their thinking.

But they persisted and asked him how he would sentence the woman.

Then he said, "Let whoever among you has never made any mistakes be the first to heave a stone at her."

And he said nothing more.

Then the orthodox looked at themselves, reproached by their consciences, and the ones in front attempted to hide behind the ones in back, and they all left quickly. And Jesus was left alone with the woman.

He looked around and saw that nobody was left. "What," he said to the woman, "is there no one here to condemn you?"

She said, "No one."

He said, "And I cannot condemn you either. Go then, and from now on, do not sin."

Beware the temptation against the fifth commandment, concerning how people consider themselves obligated only to do good to their fellow countrymen and consider other nations to be enemies.

One legalist wanted to tempt Jesus and said, "What should I do in order to receive true life?"

Jesus said, "You know. Love your father God and love your brother under your father God as well, no matter whose countryman he may be."

And the legalist said, "It would be good if there were no distinction between nations, but how am I supposed to love the enemies of my nation?"

And Jesus said, "There once was a Jew. He was struck by tragedy: attacked, robbed and tossed to the side of the road. A Jewish priest happened by, took a look at the beaten man and continued past. A Jewish Levite happened by, took a look at the beaten man and continued past. A man from a foreign, enemy nation happened by next, a Samaritan. This Samaritan saw the Jew and did not think about the feelings of Samaritans toward Jews, and simply felt sorry for the beaten Jew. He washed him, bandaged his wounds, and took him to an inn on his donkey. He paid money to the innkeeper for him and promised to stop by and pay any additional fees for him.

"You should conduct yourself the same way with foreign nations, with those who consider you nothing, those who may attack you; then you will receive true life."

Jesus said, "The world loves its own, but hates God's. Therefore, the people of the world—priests, dogmatists, and rulers—will torment those who do the will of the father. And I will soon go to Jerusalem and they will torment and kill me, but my spirit cannot be killed, it will go on living."

Having heard that Jesus would be tortured and killed in Jerusalem, Peter became distressed, took Jesus by the hand and said to him, "If that's the case, then it would be better not to go to Jerusalem."

Then Jesus said to Peter, "Do not say this. What you are saying, that is a temptation. If, for my sake, you are scared of torture and death, then that means that you are not thinking of the divine, of the spirit. You are thinking of what concerns man."

And, having called together a group of people with his students, Jesus said, "Whoever wants to live according to my teaching, let him renounce mortal life and be ready for all possible suffering in the flesh, because whoever fears for his mortal life will destroy his true life, and whoever neglects his mortal life will preserve his true life."

And they did not understand this. Then the old believers arrived and he explained to everyone what he meant by true life and awakening from death. The old believers said that after the death of the flesh there would be no more life.

They said, "How can everyone be resurrected from the dead? If everyone were resurrected, then those who were resurrected would have no room to live together. Now, we had seven brothers.

The first took a wife and then died. The wife then married the second brother, and that one died, she married the third, and he died, and so on until the seventh. So, how can these seven brothers live together with one wife if they are all going to be resurrected?"

Jesus said to them, "You are either trying to confuse things intentionally, or you do not understand what the awakening of life consists of. People in this life take wives and husbands. Those who serve eternal life and awake from death do not take husbands or wives, because they can no longer die. They are united with the father.

"In your scriptures it is written that God said, 'I am the God of Abraham and Jacob.' And God said this when Abraham and Jacob had already died, in the people's understanding. It would seem then that those who die, in people's understanding, are living in God's understanding. If God exists and he does not die, then those who are with God are always living. Awakening from death is life within the will of the father. For the father there is no time and therefore when you fulfill the father's will, and align your will with him, you can also leave time and death behind."

Having heard this, the orthodox were helpless to come up with anything that could force him into silence, so they united with the old believers and they all began to probe Jesus together.

And one of the orthodox said, "Teacher! In your opinion, what is the most important commandment in all of the law?"

The orthodox believed that Jesus would make a legal error in his answer.

But Jesus said, "The most important commandment is to love with all your soul the Lord under whose power we all live. The other arises from it: Love your neighbor, since that same Lord is within him. Everything that is written in all of your books can be found in this."

And Jesus said further, "In your opinion, what is the Christ? What is he, somebody's son?"

They said, "In our opinion, Christ is the son of David."

Then he said to them, "How could David call Christ his Lord? Christ is not David's son or anyone's son, but Christ is that very Lord, the master of us all, whom we recognize within ourselves, as our life. Christ is the knowledge within us."

And Jesus said, "Keep watch, beware of how the orthodox teachers leaven their words. Beware also the leavening of the old believers and the leavening of the government. But more than anything else, beware the leavening of the self-proclaimed orthodox, because within them is the greatest deception."

And when the people understood what he was speaking of, he said, "Be very wary of the scribes—the self-proclaimed orthodox. Beware them because they have stepped into the position of the prophet who announces the will of God to the people. They have, of their own will, taken on themselves the authority to preach the will of God to the people. They preach words, but do nothing. And it happens that they only say, 'Do this and do that,' but there is nothing to do because they do not do anything good, all they do is talk. They tell you what you are not allowed to do. And they themselves do nothing. They only attempt to retain for themselves the authority of the teacher, and in order to do so they attempt to make a display: they get dressed up and make themselves impressive.

"So? You should know that no one ought to call themselves a teacher or pastor. The self-proclaimed orthodox call themselves teachers and by doing so they block you from entering the kingdom of heaven and do not enter it themselves, either. These orthodox teachers believe that one can be brought to God through external ordinances and oaths. And, like blind men, they do not see that the external is meaningless, that all things are within the soul of man. They perform the easiest, most superficial actions, but they neglect to perform what is necessary and most difficult: love, charity and truth.

"They would prefer to satisfy the law on the outside and to lead others to the law on the outside. And due to this they are like decorated coffins, on the exterior they seem clean, but inside there is something atrocious. On the outside they respect the saints and the martyrs. But in reality, they are the very ones who torture and murder the saints. They were before and are now the enemies of goodness. All of the evil in the world comes from them because they hide goodness and promote evil in the place of good. You must fear the self-proclaimed pastors more than anything else.

"You know yourselves that every error can be corrected. But if people are deceived in what constitutes goodness, then that error cannot be corrected. And that is what the self-proclaimed pastors do."

And Jesus said, "I wanted to unite all the people here in Jerusalem into a single knowledge of true goodness, but the local people are only capable of punishing teachers of goodness. And therefore they remain the same non-believers as they were before and they will not come to know the true God, so long as they do not lovingly accept his knowledge."

And Jesus went away from the temple.

Then his students said to him, "Well, what about this temple of God with all of its decorations that people have brought into it as offerings to God?"

And Jesus said, "Truly I tell you that this temple, with all of its decorations, will be destroyed and nothing will remain of it. There is only one temple of God and that is the heart of people when they love one another."

And they asked him, "When will there be such a temple?"

And Jesus said to them, "It will not be soon. For a long time still even my teaching will be used to deceive people and there will be wars and disturbances because of it. And there will be great lawlessness and there will be little love. But when the true teaching is spread to all people, there will be an end of evil and temptation."

Chapter Ten

THE STRUGGLE WITH
TEMPTATIONS

And therefore, in order to not fall into temptation, one should be united with the father every hour of one's life.

AND LEAD US NOT INTO TEMPTATION

The Jews see that Jesus's teaching allows a place for government, faith and nationhood, and consequently they see that there is no way for them to refute his teaching, so they decide to kill him. His innocence and the demands of justice slow them, but the chief priest Caiaphus invents an argument that allows them to kill Jesus.

Caiaphus says, "We do not need to reason out whether this man is just or unjust. We just need to reason out the following: do we or do we not want our nation to remain an independent Jewish nation, or do we want it to be destroyed and scattered? This will happen if we let the man continue and do not kill him." This argument resolves the issue and the orthodox condemn Jesus to death, stirring up the people to capture him as soon as he appears in Jerusalem.

Jesus, although he knows about this, comes to Jerusalem for the Passover holiday. The students attempt to convince him not to go, but Jesus says, "What the orthodox want to do to me cannot change the truth. If I see a light, I know where I am and where I am going. Only he who does not know truth can be afraid or have any doubt about the future. Only the one who does not see can falter." And he goes to Jerusalem.

Along the way, he stops in Bethany, where Mary anoints him with a bottle of expensive oil. Knowing that a quick death of the flesh awaits him, Jesus tells the students, as they rebuke Mary for pouring such expensive oil on him, that the balm she had poured out was to prepare his body for death.

As Jesus enters Jerusalem, crowds of people meet him and follow after him, which convinces the orthodox even more of the necessity of killing him. They await an opportunity to apprehend him, and Jesus knows that. He also knows that even the slightest incautious word against the law would give them reason to execute him. Despite this, he goes to the temple and again announces that the Jews' former method of worship of sacrifices and libations is false. His teaching, based on the prophets, is such that the orthodox still cannot find any blatant violation of the law, by which they might have been able to condemn him to death.

There are gentiles at the celebration, and hearing the teaching of Jesus, they ask to speak with Jesus. The students become frightened that this conversation with gentiles will compromise Jesus and upset the crowd, but they decide to inform him of the gentiles' wish. Hearing this, Jesus is confused. He understands that preaching before the gentiles would clearly demonstrate his rejection of the entire Jewish law and provide an angle for the orthodox to accuse him of wrongdoing. He also knows that his calling is to explain to people their unity as the sons of the one father, free from any distinctions of faith. Therefore he says, "Just as the wheat kernel must be destroyed in order for it to bear fruit, man must give away his mortal life in order to bear spiritual fruit. Whoever preserves his mortal life will be deprived of true life, but whoever does not care for the flesh will receive true life. I am confused by what awaits me, but I have made it to this moment in life, so why should I not do now what I am called to?"

Addressing the people, both gentiles and Jews, Jesus speaks openly about what he had only spoken of in secret to Nicodemus. He says, "All the varied faiths should be completely changed and all human power structures should be destroyed. You must come to understand man exclusively as the son of the father of life, and this knowledge will destroy all human divisions and unite all people as one." To the Jews' accusations he says, "I do not teach any sort of new faith, I just teach what everyone knows within themselves. Everyone knows that life is given to them and to all people by the father of life. My teaching simply consists of loving the life that the father gives to all people."

Many of the simple people believe Jesus; the important and high-ranking ones do not believe since they are focused on the temporal meaning of his words. They decided not to seize him in the Jerusalem daylight, but somewhere in secret. One of the twelve students, Judas Iscariot, comes to them, and they bribe him to lead their men to Jesus when he is not surrounded by the people.

Jesus and the students celebrate the first night of Passover and Judas, thinking that Jesus does not know of his treachery, accompanies them. But Jesus knows that Judas has betrayed him and when they sit down to the table, Jesus breaks bread and offers each of the students a piece and gives them each wine from a cup, treating Judas no differently than the others. Not naming anyone, he says, "One of you will spill my blood, but I have fed him and given him drink and washed his feet. I do this in order to teach you how to behave with those who do evil to you." The students all ask which of them is the traitor, but Jesus does not name him. When it had grown dark, Jesus points to Judas and commands him to leave. Judas stands from the table and runs so no one could stop him. Then Jesus said, "To exalt the son of man means to be as good as the father is, not merely to those that love us, but to all people, including those who do evil to us. Do as I have been doing and as you have just seen me do. I give you one commandment: love people. That is my whole teaching: always love people, until the end."

Jesus becomes frightened and goes with the students by night to a garden, in order to hide. He grows sad as the students discuss how they will defend themselves. He goes into a deserted place and prays, prompting the students to do the same; but they do not understand him. Jesus says,

"My father, spirit! End this struggle with temptation inside me. Make me strong enough to fulfill your will. I do not seek my own will, to defend my mortal life, but I seek your will, to refrain from opposing evil." The students still do not understand him. He says to them, "Do not think about the flesh, but try to lift your spirits. There is power in the spirit, but the flesh has no power." At another point he says, "My father! If suffering is unavoidable, then let it be. But even in suffering I have one desire, that your will be satisfied and not mine." The students do not understand. And after more struggle with temptation, he finally conquers it, saying to the students, "Now it has been decided, you may be at peace. I will not struggle, but will offer myself into the hands of the people of this world."

After this, the orthodox bishops began to investigate Jesus with all their resources, in order to somehow find a way to destroy him. They gathered into a council and began their examination.

They said, "We need to stop this man somehow. He proves his teachings in such a way that if we do not stop him, everyone will believe in him and give up our faith. Already now, half the people have come to believe in him. But if the Jews believe in his teaching that all people are the sons of one father and are brothers, that in our Hebrew nation there is nothing special to separate us from other nations, then the Romans will completely overtake us and there will be no more Hebrew kingdom."

And the orthodox bishops and scholars were in council for a long time and could not think of what they ought to do. They could not come to a decision on killing him. And then one of them, Caiaphus, who was the chief priest that year, came up with the following argument. He said to them, "We must remember this: it is useful to kill one man so that a whole nation does not perish. If we leave this man alone, then the nation will perish, I can predict that for you, therefore it is better to kill him. Even if the nation does not perish, at the very least it will be scattered and lose its unity of faith if we do not kill Jesus. Therefore it is better to kill him."

And when Caiaphus said this, everyone agreed that there was nothing else to think about and that they must not fail to kill Jesus. They would have taken Jesus and killed him right then, but he hid from them in the desert.

And the Passover holiday approached. At that time, many people descended on Jerusalem for celebration. And the orthodox bishops counted on the fact that Jesus would come with the people to the celebration. And they announced among the people that if anyone saw Jesus, they should bring him to them.

It happened that six days before Passover Jesus said to his students, "Let us go to Jerusalem."

And he set off with them.

And his students said to him, "Do not go to Jerusalem; the bishops have now decided to beat you with stones. If you go, they will kill you."

And Jesus said to them, "I cannot fear anything, because I live in the light of knowledge. And just as any man who walks during the day and not during the night, in order not to stumble, likewise, every man can live by knowledge in order to not doubt or fear anything. Only the one who lives by the flesh can doubt and fear; for the one who lives by knowledge, there is nothing doubtful, nothing frightening."

And Jesus came to the village of Bethany, not far from Jerusalem, to visit Martha and Mary. And the sisters made dinner for him there. And when he sat down to dinner, Martha served him. And Mary took a quart of expensive, pure, fragrant oil and poured it out onto Jesus's feet and wiped it with her hair.

And when the smell of the oil had spread throughout the house,

Judas Iscariot said, "Mary has wasted that expensive oil in vain. It would have been better to sell that oil for three hundred grivna and give it to the poor."

And Jesus said, "You will always have the poor with you, but soon, I will not be with you. She has done well, she has prepared my body for burial."

In the morning Jesus went to Jerusalem. Many people were there for the celebration. And when they discovered Jesus, they surrounded him, began to tear branches from the trees and cast their clothing into the street for him and everyone shouted, "Here he is, our true king, the one who taught us of the true God."

Jesus sat on a donkey and rode it behind the people as they ran ahead of him, shouting. And that is how Jesus entered Jerusalem.

And when he entered this way into the city, all of the residents became upset and asked, "Who is that?"

Those that knew him, answered, "That is Jesus, the prophet from Nazareth of Galilee."

And Jesus entered the temple and again drove out all of the merchants and buyers.

And the orthodox priests saw all of this and said to each other, "Look what this man is doing. All of the people are following after him."

But they did not dare to take him directly from the people because they saw that the people supported him, so they began to plot a way to take him by cunning.

Meanwhile Jesus was in the temple, teaching the people. In this group of people, apart from Jews there were Greek gentiles. The Greeks had heard of Jesus's teaching and understood from it that he taught truth not only for the Jews, but for all people. And they also wanted to be his students, so they told Philip about this and Philip told Andrew. The students were afraid to bring Jesus together with the Greeks. They were afraid that the people would become embittered toward Jesus for not acknowledging the difference between the Jews and other nations, so they avoided telling Jesus for a long time, but then they both told him together.

Hearing that the Greeks wanted to become his students, Jesus became confused. He knew that the people would hate him for not making a distinction between the Jews and the gentiles, for acknowledging himself to be the same as the gentiles.

He said, "The time has come to explain what I mean by the son of man. And it may mean that I will perish for not making a distinction between the Jews and the gentiles in my explanation of this teaching, but I will speak the truth. A wheat kernel will bring forth fruit only after it dies itself. Whoever loves his mortal life will lose his true life, but whoever neglects his mortal life preserves it in eternal life. Whoever wants to work for my teaching, let him do as I do. And whoever does as I do will be rewarded by my father. My soul is struggling now: should I give into the considerations of temporal life or should I fulfill the father's will now, at this moment. And now that the hour has arrived, and I am still living, can I really say, 'Father, save me from the thing that I should do!'? No, I cannot say that just because I happen to be living now. And so I say, 'Father! Show yourself in me!'"

And Jesus said, "From now on the world of people is condemned to death. From now on the thing that controls this world will be destroyed. And when the son of man is glorified above earthly life, then he will unite all people as one."

And then the Jews said to him, "We understand according to the law that there is an eternal Christ; how is it that you say that the son of man should be glorified? What does it mean to glorify the son of man?"

At this, Jesus answered them, "To glorify the son of man means to live by the light of knowledge that is within you. To glorify the son of man above the earth means to believe in the light, insofar as there is light, in order to be a son of knowledge. He who believes in my teaching does not believe in me, but in that spirit who gave life to the world. And he who understands my teaching understands that spirit who gave life to the world. My teaching is the light of life, which has led people out of darkness.

"If somebody hears my words and does not fulfill them, then I do not blame him, since I came not to condemn but to save. He who does not receive my words is not condemned by my teaching, but by the knowledge that lives within it. That is what condemns him, because I have not spoken my own words, but have spoken what my father, the spirit living within me, inspired me to speak. What I say is only what I was told by the spirit of knowledge. And what I teach is true life."

And having said this, Jesus left and again hid from the bishops.

And of those who had heard these words from Jesus, many of the strong and wealthy people believed in Jesus's teaching, but they were afraid to admit this before the bishops because not one of the bishops admitted that they believed. This was because they were accustomed to judging by men's standards and not by God's.

After Jesus had hidden, the bishops and the elders again gathered at Caiaphus's courtyard. And they began to determine how they might apprehend Jesus in secret, take him from the people and kill him. They were afraid to apprehend him in the open.

And one of the twelve students of Jesus, Judas Iscariot, came to them at their conference and said, "If you want to apprehend Jesus secretly, so that the people don't see, then I will find a time when very few people will be with him and I will show you where he is so that you can take him. What will you give me for this?"

They promised to give him thirty rubles for this service. He agreed, and from then on began looking for a time when he could lead the bishops to Jesus, so that they could take him.

Meanwhile, Jesus was hiding from the people, and only his students were with him. When the first part of the holiday, the celebration of unleavened bread, arrived, the students said to Jesus, "Where are we going to celebrate Passover?"

And Jesus said, "Go into the village somewhere and stop by someone's house and say that we have no time to prepare Passover and ask him to let us in to observe Passover."

The students did just that—they went and asked a man in the village and he let them in. Then they entered and sat at the table: Jesus and the twelve students; and Judas was with them.

Jesus knew that Judas Iscariot had already promised to turn him over to face his death, but he did not expose Judas and did not avenge himself on Judas for this, and just as he had taught his students love his whole life, now he likewise reproached Judas only with love.

When all the twelve had sat down to the table, he looked at them and said, "Among you sits someone that has betrayed me. Yes, he who drinks and eats with me will also destroy me."

He said nothing more, and they could not determine who it was that he was referring to, so they began their dinner. When they had begun to eat, Jesus took the bread, broke it into twelve parts, gave each of the twelve students a piece and said, "Take and eat—this is my body."

And then he poured out a cup of wine, gave it to the students and said, "Drink from this cup, all of you."

And when they had all drunk, he said, "This is my blood. I spill it so people can know that my will is to forgive others their sins. Because I will soon die and I will no longer be with you in this world, but will be united with you only in the kingdom of heaven."

After that Jesus stood up from the table, wrapped a towel around himself like a belt, and took a pitcher of water and began to wash all of the students' feet.

And he came to Peter, but Peter said, "How is it that you can be washing my feet?"

Jesus said to him, "It seems strange to you that I wash your feet, but you must understand now why I do this. I do it because although you are clean, albeit not entirely so, among you sits my betrayer, to whom I gave bread with my own hands as well as wine, and whose feet I want to wash."

And when Jesus had washed all of their feet, he again sat down and said, "Have you understood why I did this? I did this so that you will do the very same for each other, always. I, your teacher, do this so that you will know how to behave with those who do evil to you. If you have understood this and will do this, then you will be blessed. When I said that one of you will betray me, I was not speaking about all of you, because only one of you whose feet I have washed and given bread to eat, just one of you will destroy me."

And having said that, Jesus became indignant in his spirit and again said, "Yes, yes, one of you will betray me."

And again the students began to look at one another and did not know who it was that he referred to. One student sat close by Jesus. Simon Peter nodded to him so that he would ask him who the traitor was. This student asked him.

Jesus said, "I will dip a piece of bread and offer it to someone, and the one to whom I offer it is the traitor."

And he offered it to Judas Iscariot, and he said to him, "Do what you will, and do it quickly."

Judas understood that he had to leave and as soon as he took the piece of bread, he left immediately. And there was no time to chase after him.

And when Judas had left, Jesus said, "Now it is clear to you, what the son of man is, now it is clear to you that if God is within him, he can be as good as God is.

"Children! I do not have long to be with you. Do not philosophize about my teaching, as I said to the orthodox, but just do as I do. I give you one new commandment: just as I have always and indefinitely loved you all, likewise you must always and indefinitely love one another. This will be the only thing that will set you apart. Only in this will you differ from other people: love one another."

And after this they went to the Mount of Olives.

Along the way Jesus said to them, "Now is the time when what is written in the scriptures will take place, that they will kill the shepherd and the sheep will all scatter. That will happen this very night. They will take me and you will all abandon me and run your separate ways."

And in answer, Peter said to him, "Even if all the others are frightened and run away, I will not deny you. I am prepared to go with you to prison and to death."

Jesus said to him, "But I tell you that when I am taken, you will turn your back on me, not once, but three times before the cocks crow this night." But Peter said that he would not turn his back; the other students said the same.

Then Jesus said to the students, "Previously I did not need anything and you did not need anything. You traveled without a bag and without extra footwear; and I had commanded you to do so. But now, if they have found me to be a lawbreaker, it has become impossible to continue that way, so we must store up everything and gather knives so that we are not destroyed in vain."

And the students said, "Here, we have two knives."

Jesus said, "Good!"

And having said that, Jesus went with the students into the Garden of Gethsemane. And as they entered the garden, Jesus said, "Let us stay here a while, I want to pray."

And approaching Peter and the two sons of Zebedee, he began to languish and to grow sorrowful, saying to them, "This is very difficult for me. I am sorrowing before death. Remain here and do not despair as I do."

And he went off a short way, laid down, prone, on the ground and began to pray, saying, "My father, the spirit! Let this be not as I want, to not die, but as you want. Even though I may die, still, for you, as the spirit, everything is possible; make it so that I do not fear death, so that there be no temptation of the flesh for me."

Then he stood, approached the students and saw that they had become depressed. And he said to them, "How is it that you do not have the power to lift your spirits for one hour, as I do? Lift your spirits so that you do not fall into the temptation of the flesh. The spirit is strong, but the flesh is weak."

And again Jesus went off a short way and again began to pray and said, "Father! If it is impossible for me to avoid suffering and I have to die, then let me die. Let your will come to pass!"

And, having said that, he again approached the students and saw that they had grown even more depressed and were on the verge of tears.

Again he went a short way off and for the third time said, "Father! Let your will come to pass."

Then he returned to the students and said to them, "Now you may be at peace and be calm, because everything has been decided, and I will turn myself over into the hands of worldly people."

Chapter Eleven

THE FAREWELL CONVERSATION

Individual life is a delusion of the flesh, it is evil.
The true life is a common life for all people.

BUT DELIVER US FROM EVIL

Feeling ready for death, Jesus prepares to turn himself in. Peter stops him and asks where he is going. Jesus answers, "I am going to where you cannot go. I am ready for death and you are still not ready for it." Peter says, "No, I am ready now to give my life for you." Jesus answers, "A man cannot promise himself for anything."

And he says to all the students, "I know that death awaits me, but I believe in the life of the father and so I am not scared. Do not be upset about my death either, but believe in the true God and in the father of life and my death will not seem so terrible to you. If I am united with the father of life, then I cannot be deprived of life. True, I do not tell you what kind and where and when my life will be after death, but I am showing you the path to true life. It is as simple as unifying yourself with the father, the source of all life. After me, your mentor will be your knowledge of truth. By fulfilling my teaching, you will always feel that you are in the truth, that the father is within you and you are in the father. And knowing that the father of life is within you, you will experience a peace which no one will be able to take from you. Therefore, if you know the truth and live it, then neither my death nor your own can trouble you.

"People imagine themselves to be separate beings, each with their own particular will for life; but that is just a delusion. The one true life is the

one that recognizes the source of life as the father's will. My teaching reveals this unity of life and imagines life not as separate branches, but as one single tree, upon which all of the different branches grow. Whoever wants to live according to their own will, like a branch torn off, will die. If you live within the father's will, then you will have all that you wish, because life is given to people for their well-being. If you fulfill my commandments you will be blessed. The commandment that expresses all of my teaching is simply that all people should love one another. Love consists of sacrificing your mortal life for others—there is no other definition for love. And when you fulfill my commandment to love, you will be doing so as free people, not as slaves. You did not accept my teaching accidentally, you accepted it because it is the one true teaching under which all people are free.

"The world's teaching is founded on doing evil to people; my teaching is to love one another. Therefore the world will hate you just as much as it has hated me. The world does not understand my teaching and therefore it will persecute you and do evil to you, assuming that in doing so it is serving God. Do not be amazed by this, just understand that this is the way it must be. The world, not understanding the true God, must drive you out and you must continue to affirm the truth.

"You will be distressed that they kill me, but they are killing me because I am affirming the truth. My death is necessary for the affirmation of truth, it will affirm you and you will understand what is a lie and what is truth. You will understand the lie behind people's belief in mortal life and lack of belief in the life of the spirit. You will understand that the truth is in union with the father and that through this the spirit can conquer the flesh. When I am no longer present in this mortal life, my spirit will be with you. But you, as all people, will not always feel the power of the spirit within you. Sometimes you will grow weak and lose the power of the spirit, you will fall into temptation, sometimes you will awaken into true life anew. You will find yourself in times of enslavement to the flesh, but this will only be temporary. You will suffer a bit and then be born again by the spirit, like

a woman suffers in the torments of childbirth but then feels joy in the birth of a person into the world. You will experience the same when your spirits are lifted after having been enslaved to the flesh. You will then feel such a blessing that you will no longer have anything else to desire. Remember that the spirit lives within you and that the one true God is the knowledge of the father's will, as I have revealed it."

Addressing himself to the spirit father, Jesus says, "I have done what you commanded me to do, I have revealed to people that you are the source of all. And they have understood me. I have taught them that they all emanate from one source of endless life and that therefore they are all one, that just as the father is within me and I am in the father, they are one with me and with the father. I also revealed to them that since you sent them lovingly into the world, they ought to live by love in the world."

———————

And Peter said to Jesus, "Where are you going?" Jesus answered, "You will not have the strength to go where I am now going. Only much later will you be going to this same place."

And Peter said, "Why do you think that I do not have the strength to go where you are going now? I will give my life for you."

And Jesus said, "You say that you will give your life for me, but you would deny me three times even before the cocks crow."

Jesus said to the students, "Do not be troubled and do not be timid, but believe in the true God of life and in my teaching. The life of the father is not the one that exists on earth; it is a different life. If there were only this life here, then I would say to you that when I die, I will be going into the bosom of Abraham and preparing a place for you there. And I will come and take you and we will be blessed together in the bosom of Abraham. But instead I am only pointing out the path toward life."

Thomas said, "But we do not know where you are going so

therefore we cannot know the path. We need to know, what will there be after death?"

Jesus said, "I cannot show you what will be there; my teaching is the path, the truth and the life. And it is impossible to unite with the father of life any other way than through my teaching. If you fulfill my teaching, then you will come to know the father."

Philip said, "But who is the father?"

And Jesus said, "The father is what gives life. I fulfill the father's will, and therefore you can understand what the father's will is by learning from my life. I live by the father and the father lives within me. And all that I say and do, it is all according to the father's will. My teaching is that I am within the father and the father is within me. If you do not understand the teaching itself, then you can observe me and my actions and through this you can understand what the father is.

"You must understand that whoever follows my teaching can accomplish the same as I can and even more because I am going to die, but he will still be living. Whoever lives according to my teaching will have all that he desires, because then the son will be the same as the father. Whatever you desire, according to my teaching, will be given to you in full. But for that to happen, you must love my teaching.

"My teaching will provide you an advocate in my place, and a comforter. This comforter will be your conscience of truth, which people of the world do not understand. But you will know it within yourself. You will never be alone if the spirit of my teaching is with you. I will die and the people of the world will not see me, but you will see me because my teaching survives and you will live by it. And then if my teaching is within you, you will come to understand that I am within the father and that the father is within me. Whoever fulfills my teaching will feel the father within himself, and my spirit will live."

Judas, the one not called Iscariot, said to him, "But why can't everyone live by the spirit of truth?"

And in answer, Jesus said, "Only the one who fulfills my teaching can be loved by the father and my spirit can take up residence only in one such as him. Whoever does not fulfill my teaching cannot be loved by my father because my teaching is not my own, but my father's. And that is all that I can say to you right now. But my spirit, the spirit of truth, which will take up residence within you after I am gone, will reveal to you everything, and you will recall and understand much of what I have just told you.

"And so, you can always be at peace in your spirit, and not with the worldly peace that the people of the world seek, but with the peace of the spirit, in whose presence you will no longer fear anything. From this, if you fulfill my teaching, then you have no reason to be distressed by my death. Like the spirit of truth, I will come to you and together with the father's conscience will take up residence in your heart. If you fulfill my teaching, then you will rejoice because in my place the father will be in your hearts, and that is better for you.

"My teaching is the tree of life. The father is he who cultivates the tree. He cleans and grooms those branches that bear fruit so that even more will grow on them. Hold to my teaching of life and life will grow within you. And just as the branch does not live of itself, but takes life from the tree, likewise you will take life from my teaching. My teaching is the tree; you are the branches. Whoever lives by my teaching of life will bear much fruit. And so, apart from my teaching there is no life.

"Whoever does not live by my teaching will shrivel and perish, and all the dry branches will be pruned and incinerated. If you live by my teaching and fulfill it, then you will have all that you desire. The will of the father is that you live the true life and receive what you desire. Just as the father gave goodness to me, likewise, I give goodness to you. Hold on to this goodness.

"I am living because the father loves me and I love the father; you must live by that same love. If you will live by this love, you will be blessed. My commandment is that you love one another as I have loved you. There is no greater love than to sacrifice your life for the love that you have toward those close to you, as I have done.

"You are equal with me if you do what I have taught you. I do not consider you to be slaves, to whom orders are given, but to be equals because I have made plain to you everything that I have come to understand from the father. You are not choosing my teaching of your own will, but because I have directed you toward the one truth, the truth that allows you all to live and have everything you desire. The entire teaching is nothing more than loving one another.

"If the world hates you, do not be amazed: it hates my teaching. If you were one with the world, then it would love you. But I have separated you from the world, and for that, it will hate you. If they drove me out, then they will drive you out. They will do this all because they do not know the true God. I have explained it to them, but they did not even want to listen to me. They did not understand my teaching because they did not understand the father. They saw my life and my life showed them their mistakes. And for that they hated me even more. The spirit of truth which will come to you will confirm this. And then you will confirm this.

"I tell you this in advance so that you won't be deceived when the persecutions fall upon you. They will turn you into outcasts. Everyone will think that by killing you they are pleasing God. They cannot avoid doing any of this because they do not understand either my teaching or the true God. I tell you all of this in advance so that you won't be amazed when this all happens.

"And so, I will go off now to that spirit which sent me. You understand now that you cannot ask me where I am going. Earlier you were distressed that I would not tell you where exactly, to what place I was going. But I tell you truly that it is good for you that I am going. If I do not die, then the spirit of truth will not appear to you, but if I die, then it will take up residence within you. It will take up residence in you and it will become clear to you what is a lie, what is truth, and what the resolution is.

"The lie is when people do not believe in the life of the spirit. The truth is that I am one with the father. And the resolution is that the power of mortal life has been destroyed. I would still tell you much more, but it is difficult for you to understand. When the spirit of truth takes up residence in you, it will show you all truth, because it will not tell you what is new or what you want to hear, but what comes from God. It will show you the way in all situations of life. It will also be from the father, just as I am from the father. Therefore it will say the same things that I say. But when I, the spirit of truth, am within you, you will not always see me. Sometimes you will, but other times you will not hear me."

And the students said to each other, "What does that mean?"

He said, "Sometimes you will see me, other times you will not see me."

"What does it mean when he says, 'Sometimes you will, sometimes you will not'?"

Jesus said to them, "You do not understand what it means that sometimes you will but other times you won't see me. You understand, as it always happens in the world, that some people are sad and grieving while others are rejoicing. You will be sad, and your sadness will turn into joy. A woman, when she gives birth, grieves when in labor, but when it ends, she doesn't remember the grief because of her joy at having brought a person into the world. Likewise, you will be sad but suddenly you will see me, the spirit of truth will enter into you and your sadness will turn into joy. And then you will no longer ask anything of me, because at that point you will have everything that you desire. At that point, everything that a man could desire in the spirit will be given to him by the father.

"Earlier, you did not ask anything from the spirit, but in the future, you may ask anything that you want from the spirit and it will come to you, so that your blessedness will be complete. Now I, as a man, cannot say this clearly to you with words, but when I live within you as the spirit of truth, I will clearly make known to you all things concerning the father. Then, everything that you ask the father in the name of the spirit will be given to you, and not by me. Your father will give it to you because he loves you for accepting my teaching. You have understood that knowledge from the father comes into the world and returns to the father from the world."

Then the students said to Jesus, "Now we have all understood and we have nothing left to ask. We believe that you come from God."

And Jesus said, "I have said all of this to you, so that you would have surety and peace in my teaching. Whatever misfortunes you may have in the world, do not fear anything because my teaching will overcome the world."

After this, Jesus lifted his eyes toward heaven and said, "My father! You gave your son freedom in life, so that he could receive true life. Life is knowing the true God, the knowledge that I have revealed. I revealed you to the people of the earth. I did the deed that you commanded me to do. I manifested your existence to the people of the earth. They were yours before as well, but according to your will I revealed the truth to them. And they came to know you.

"They have understood that all they have, even their life, comes only from you. And I taught them, not from myself, that both they and I issue from you. I plead to you for those that have acknowledged you. They have understood that all that is mine is yours, and all that is yours is mine.

"I am now no longer in the world, but am returning to you; but they are in the world and therefore I ask you, father, to keep your knowledge within them. I am not asking that you take them out of the world, but that you save them from evil. I ask you to confirm them in your truth. Your knowledge is truth.

"My father! I desire for them to be the same as I am, for them to understand in the same way that I do, that true life began before the creation of the world. That they will all be one, as you, father, are within me and I within you, and that they will be within us as one. I am within them, and you are within me, so that we all can be united as one and so that people understand that they were not born of themselves, but that you sent them into the world lovingly, just as you sent me.

"Righteous father! The world did not come to know you on its own, but I came to know you, and they came to know you through me. And I explained to them what you are. You are what causes the same love to appear within them as the love you gave me. You gave them life, so, accordingly, you loved them. I taught them that they must remember this and love you, so that the love you gave them will return from them to you."

Chapter Twelve

THE SPIRIT'S VICTORY OVER THE FLESH

And therefore, there can be no evil for the man
within the father's will, who lives a life in common
with others and not his own individual life. The death
of the flesh is unification with the father.

FOR THINE IS THE KINGDOM AND THE
POWER AND THE GLORY.

When Jesus finishes his speech to his students, he stands and instead of fleeing or defending himself, goes to meet Judas, who is leading the soldiers to apprehend him. Jesus approaches him and asks him why he had come. But Judas does not answer and the group of soldiers surrounds Jesus. Peter rushes to defend his teacher and begins to fight with a knife; Jesus stops Peter and says that whoever fights with a knife would himself perish from the knife, and commands him to surrender the knife. He gives himself up to those that had come to take him. All of the students scatter and Jesus remained alone.

The chief of the soldiers commands that Jesus be bound and brought to Caiaphus, the current bishop and the one who had come up with the argument that had justified the killing of Jesus. Jesus, feeling himself to be within the will of the father, does not resist, and does not fear as they lead him away. But Peter, who had just promised Jesus that he would not deny him, and that he would die for him, when he sees that Jesus is going to be executed, is scared that he would be executed as well, and disavows any connection to Jesus and leaves. Only afterwards, when the cock crows, does Peter understand everything that Jesus had told him. He understands that there are two temptations of the flesh: fear and violence, and that Jesus had been struggling with them when he prayed in the garden and invited the students to pray with him. He understands that he has now fallen into both of these temptations: he had wanted to defend the truth with violence, and he had not withstood the fear of suffering in the flesh by denying his teacher.

Caiaphus begins to interrogate Jesus, to see what his teaching consisted of. But Jesus knows that Caiaphus is not interested in the meaning of his teaching but is simply looking to accuse him, and so does not answer, but says, "If you want to know my teaching, speak with those that listened to it and understood it." Jesus is beaten for this. Witnesses are brought in to demonstrate that Jesus had boasted about destroying the Jewish faith.

The bishop commands, "Tell me, are you the Christ, the son of God?" Jesus says, "Yes, I am a man, the son of God, and now, when you torment me, you will see that a man can be equal with God." The bishop is overjoyed with these words because they proved Jesus's guilt. The judges condemn him to death. And all of the people throw themselves at Jesus and beat him, spitting in his face and swearing at him. He is silent.

The Jews did not have the authority to condemn people to death, so they bring Jesus to the Roman leader Pilate, for him to sentence Jesus to death. Pilate asks them why they want to kill Jesus. They say, "Because he is an evil man." Pilate says, "If he is an evil man, then judge him according to your law." They say, "We want you to execute him because he is guilty before the Roman Caesar: he is an insurgent, he plants mutiny among the people, he forbids them to pay taxes to Caesar, calling himself the Jewish king." Pilate calls Jesus to him and says, "What does this mean that you are the Jewish king?" Jesus says, "Do you want to know exactly what my kingdom means? Or are you asking me only for the sake of appearances?" Pilate says, "I am not a Jew and it is all the same to me whether you call *yourself the Jewish king or not; I am asking you what kind of man you are and for what reason they are saying that you are a king?" Jesus says, "It is true that I call myself a king, but my kingdom is not an earthly kingdom, it is a heavenly one. Earthly kings kill each other, make battles and command troops, but you see: they have bound me and beaten me, but I am not opposing them. I am a king of heaven, I am all-powerful in spirit. Everyone who lives according to truth is free and is therefore a king. I live and teach only in order to reveal the truth to people that they are free in spirit." Pilate says, "You teach truth, but no one knows what truth is. Everyone has their own truth." Having said that he turned and walked away from Jesus, back to the Jews.*

Pilate says, "I have not found anything criminal in this man. Why execute him?" The bishops say, "We must execute him because he is inciting the people to rebellion." Then Pilate interrogates Jesus in front of the bishops; but Jesus, seeing that this interrogation was only for the sake of form, does not answer. Then Pilate says, "I cannot condemn him by myself; take him to Herod."

At Herod's court, Jesus likewise says nothing and does not answer the accusations of the bishops, and Herod, taking Jesus to be a fool, commands them to dress him in red clothing for comic effect and send him back to Pilate. Pilate is sorry for Jesus. He tries to convince the bishops to forgive Jesus in consideration of the holiday at least, but the bishops would not relent and they all, with the people behind them, cry for Jesus to be crucified on a cross. They say, "He is guilty of calling himself the son of God." Pilate calls Jesus to him again and asks him, "What does it mean that you call yourself the son of God? Who are you?" Jesus does not answer. Then Pilate says, "How is it that you do not answer me when I have the power to either execute or free you?" Jesus responds, "You do not have any power over me. Power comes only from above." And Pilate, for the third time, tries to convince the Jews to release Jesus, but they say to him, "If you do not execute this man, whom we have shown to be an insurgent against Caesar, then you yourself are no friend to Caesar, you are an enemy." And hearing these words, Pilate capitulates and commands that Jesus be executed. Jesus is undressed, cut open and again dressed in ridiculous clothing; they beat him, laugh, and swear at him. Then they give him a cross to carry and command him to go to the place of execution and there they crucify him on a cross.

As Jesus hangs on the cross, all of the people curse him. He answers these curses by saying, "Father! Do not condemn them: they do not know what they are doing." And then, when he is close to death, he says, "My father! I offer my soul to your power." And bowing his head, he releases his spirit.

———————

And after that Jesus said, "Now stand up and let us go, the one who betrays me is already approaching."

As soon as he said this, Judas, one of the twelve students, suddenly appeared and with him, a large group of people with clubs and knives.

Judas said to them, "I will take you to where he is with his students. And so that you can distinguish him from all the others, watch for this: whomever I kiss first, that will be him."

And right away he went up to Jesus and said, "Hello, teacher!"

And he kissed him.

And Jesus said to him, "Friend! Why are you here?"

Then the guards surrounded Jesus, wanting to take him.

And at this point Peter took the knife of the bishops' servant and severed the man's ear.

Jesus said, "There is no need to oppose evil. Leave it alone."

And to Peter, he said, "Give the knife back to the one you took it from. Whoever takes up the sword will perish by the sword."

After this Jesus turned to the whole crowd and said, "Why have you come to me, like bandits, with weapons? I have been among you every day, after all, at the temple, teaching you, and you did not take me then. Your time has come as has the power of darkness."

Then, having seen that he had been taken, all the students scattered.

Then the chief commanded the soldiers to take Jesus and bind him. The soldiers bound him and took him first to Anan, who was the father-in-law of Caiaphus. Caiaphus was the high priest for the current year and lived in the same courtyard as Anan. This was the same Caiaphus who had devised the way to destroy Jesus. He had proposed that it would be beneficial for the nation to destroy Jesus because if they did not destroy Jesus, it would be bad for the whole nation.

And Jesus was taken into the courtyard of the home where the high priest lived. When Jesus was being taken there, one of his students, Peter, followed after him at some distance and saw where he was being taken. When they took Jesus into the courtyard of the high priest, Peter went in as well to see how it all would end.

And a certain girl in the courtyard saw Peter and said to him, "You were with Jesus the Galilean also."

Peter was scared that he would be condemned as well, so he loudly said, in front of all the people, "I do not know what you are saying."

Then, when Jesus had been taken into the home, Peter went with all the people into the inner porch. On the porch, there was a woman keeping warm by a fire as Peter approached.

The woman glanced at Peter and said to the other people, "Look at this man, it seems to me that he was with Jesus the Nazarene also."

Peter was scared even more and swore that he had never been with Jesus and did not know who this man Jesus was.

A short time later, some people came to Peter and said, "But by all appearances you were one of these insurgents. We can tell by your accent that you are from Galilee."

Then Peter began to swear and vow that he never knew and had never seen Jesus. And just as he said this, the cock crowed. And Peter remembered the words that Jesus had said when Peter swore that even if all the others denied him, he would never deny him, "Before the cock crows to end this night, you will deny me three times." And Peter left the courtyard and cried bitterly. He cried because he had failed to raise his spirit high enough to avoid falling into temptation. He had fallen into the one temptation of violence, when he had begun to defend Jesus, and into the other temptation of fear before death when he had denied Jesus.

And the orthodox bishops, dogmatists and leaders all gathered together at the high priest's home. And when they had all come together, they brought in Jesus, and the high priest asked him what his teaching was and who his students were.

And Jesus answered, "I have always spoken openly to the world and I am speaking that way now. I have never hidden anything from anyone and am not hiding anything now. Why is it that you are asking me? Ask those that listened to me and understood my teaching. They will tell you."

When Jesus had said this, one of the bishops' servants hit Jesus in the face, saying, "Do you know who you are speaking to? Is that how one ought to speak to a bishop?"

Jesus said, "If I said something wrong, tell me that I said something wrong. But if I did not say anything wrong, then you have no reason to hit me."

The orthodox bishops attempted to accuse Jesus and at first they could not find the sort of evidence that would be required in order to sentence him. Then they found two witnesses.

These witnesses said of Jesus, "We heard with our own ears

what this man said: 'I,' he said, 'will destroy this man-made temple of yours and in three days will build another temple to God—one made without human hands.'"

But these pieces of evidence were still not enough to convict him.

Therefore the bishop decided to challenge Jesus and said, "What is keeping you from answering their statements?"

Jesus was silent and did not say anything.

Then the bishop said to him, "Then tell us, are you the Christ, the son of God?"

Jesus answered him by saying, "Yes, I am the Christ, the son of God. And you yourselves will see now that the son of man is equal to God."

Then the bishop shouted, "You are blaspheming against God! And now we have no need for additional evidence. We all can hear now that you are a blasphemer."

And the bishop turned to the council and said, "Now you have heard for yourselves that he blasphemes against God. What sentence will you give him for this crime?"

And they all said, "We sentence him to death."

And then all of the people and the guards fell upon Jesus and began to spit in his face and to slap his cheeks and scratch him.

They bound his eyes, hit him about the face and asked, "Well now, you prophet, take a guess: who is it that hit you?"

And Jesus was silent.

Having humiliated him, they took the bound man to Pontius Pilate, leading him to the administration.

Pilate, the ruler, came out to them and asked, "What do you accuse this man of doing?"

They said, "This man does evil, and that is why we have brought him to you."

And Pilate said to them, "But if he does evil to you, then you should judge him yourselves according to your law." But they said, "We have brought him to you because we want you to execute him; we are not allowed to kill anyone."

And that is how what Jesus had expected came to pass. He had said that he must be prepared to die on a cross at the hands of the Romans, and not a natural death and not at the hands of the Jews.

When Pilate had asked them what they were accusing him of doing, they said that he was guilty of inciting the people to rebellion, that he had forbidden them from paying their taxes to Caesar and that he presented himself as the Christ and a king.

Pilate listened to them and commanded that Jesus be brought to him in his chambers.

When Jesus came in, Pilate said to him, "Are you this Jewish king?"

Jesus said to him, "Do you really suspect that I am a king or are you just repeating what the others have told you?"

Pilate said, "I am not a Jew. Accordingly, you cannot be my king, but your own people have brought you to me. What sort of man are you?"

Jesus said, "I am a king, but my kingdom is not an earthly one. If I were an earthly king, my subjects would be fighting for me and not surrendering to the bishops. But as you can see, my kingdom is not an earthly one."

Pilate said to this, "But all the same, you consider yourself a king?"

Jesus said, "Not only I, but you also must consider me a king. I make this point only in order to reveal to everyone the truth of the kingdom of heaven. And everyone who lives by the truth is a king."

Pilate said, "You say: truth. What is truth?" And having said that, he turned and went back to the bishops. He went out to them and said, "In my opinion, this man has not done anything wrong."

But the bishops insisted, saying that he had done considerable evil and had incited the people to rebellion, that he had incited all of Judea, starting in Galilee.

Then Pilate began to question Jesus in front of the bishops, but Jesus would not answer.

Pilate said to him, "Don't you see how they are condemning you, why do you not explain yourself?"

But Jesus continued to be silent and did not say another word, and as a result, Pilate was amazed.

Pilate remembered that Galilee was under the power of King Herod and asked, "Is he from Galilee?"

They said to him, "Yes."

Then he said, "If he is from Galilee, then he is under Herod's jurisdiction. I will send the man to him."

Herod was in Jerusalem at that time, so Pilate, in order to extricate himself from these people, sent Jesus to Herod. Herod was very happy to see Jesus when he was led in. He had heard much about him and wanted to find out what sort of man he was.

Herod called him in and began to question him about everything that he wanted to know; Jesus did not answer him anything. And the bishops and teachers, just as they had done with Pilate, accused Jesus harshly before Herod and said that he was an insurgent. And Herod considered Jesus to be a foolish man, so, in order to ridicule him, he commanded that Jesus be dressed in a red garment and then sent him back again to Pilate.

Herod felt satisfied that Pilate respected him, having sent Jesus to him for judgment, and because of this the two made peace, whereas previously they had been in a dispute. And after Jesus had been brought back to Pilate, Pilate called the bishops and Jewish leaders in again.

And he said to them, "You already brought this man to me because he incites the people to rebellion, and I questioned him in front of all of you and saw no sign of him being an insurgent. I sent him with you to Herod, and now, as you can see, they did not find anything dangerous about him there either. So, in my opinion, there is no reason to sentence him to death, but it would be better to punish him and let him go."

And when the bishops heard this, they all shouted, "No, execute him, execute him in the Roman style, stretch him out on a cross."

Pilate listened to this and said to the bishops, "Well, all right, but consider your tradition of forgiving one criminal every year for the Passover holiday. Here, in my prison sits Barabbas, the murderer and insurgent. So, one of these two must be acquitted: should it be Jesus or Barabbas?"

Pilate wanted to help Jesus, but the bishops had influenced the people so that they all shouted, "Barabbas! Barabbas!"

And Pilate said, "So what should I do with Jesus?"

Again, they shouted, "Hang him on a cross as the Romans do, hang him on a cross!"

And Pilate began to try to persuade them. He said, "For what reason are you so opposed to him? He has done nothing that would warrant sentencing to death. He has done no evil toward you. I will release him because I see no guilt in him."

The bishops and their servants shouted, "Crucify, crucify him!"

And Pilate said to them, "If that is how it must be, then take him yourself and crucify him, but I see no guilt in him."

And the bishops answered, "We demand what the law requires. According to the law, he must be executed because he has made himself the son of God."

When Pilate heard these words, he became confused because he did not know what these words, the son of God, meant.

And, returning into his chambers, Pilate again called Jesus to him and asked him, "Who are you and where do you come from?"

But Jesus did not answer him.

Then Pilate said, "Why are you not answering me? Don't you see that you are here in my power and that I can either crucify you or release you?"

Jesus answered him, "You do not have any power. Power comes only from above."

Nevertheless, Pilate still wanted to release Jesus, and said, "How is it that you want to crucify your king?"

But the Jews said, "If you release Jesus, then you are demonstrating by doing so that you are a disloyal servant to Caesar, because this man who calls himself a king is an enemy to Caesar. Our king is Caesar! Crucify him."

And when Pilate had heard these words, he understood that it had already become impossible for him to avoid executing Jesus.

So Pilate went to the Jews and took some water, washed his hands and said, "I am not to blame for the blood of this righteous man."

And the whole crowd shouted, "Let his blood be on our hands and our children's."

And this is how the bishops overwhelmed him.

Then Pilate sat down in his sitting place, and commanded that Jesus be flogged first.

When they had flogged him, the soldiers who had done the flogging placed a wreath on his head and put a stick in his hand and threw a red cloak on his back and began to ridicule him: they bowed, laughing, at his feet and said, "Rejoice, it is the Jewish king!"

But then they beat him on his cheeks and on his head and spat in his face.

The bishops shouted, "Crucify him! Our king is Caesar. Crucify him."

Then Pilate commanded that he be crucified.

They then took the red garments off of Jesus, put his own garments back on him and commanded him to carry the cross to the place called Golgotha, so that they could crucify him there. And he carried his cross to the place called Golgotha.

And there they stretched (crucified) Jesus on a cross, and two other men as well; the two on either side and Jesus in the middle.

When they had crucified Jesus, he said, "Father! absolve them: they do not know what they are doing."

And once Jesus had been hung on the cross, the people surrounded him and swore at him.

They approached, shook their heads at him and said, "Now then, you wanted to destroy the temple of Jerusalem and rebuild it again in three days. So now, free yourself: get down from the cross."

And the bishops and pastors stood there and made fun of him, saying, "He saved others, but he cannot save himself. Now show us that you are the Christ, come down from the cross and then we will believe in you. He said that he is the son of God and said that God would not abandon him. Well, what now? God seems to have abandoned him."

And the people, along with the bishops and soldiers, swore at him and even one of those being crucified alongside him cursed him as well.

One of the thieves, cursing, said to him, "If you are the Christ, why not save yourself and us."

But the other thief heard this and said, "You have no respect for God: you are hanging on a cross yourself and you are still cursing at an innocent man. We are being executed for something we have done, but this man did not do anything wrong."

And turning to Jesus, this thief said to him, "Lord! Remember me in your kingdom."

And Jesus said to him, "And now you will be blessed along with me."

In the ninth hour, Jesus, entirely exhausted, spoke out loudly, "Eli, Eli, lama sabachthami?" That means: My God, my God, to what have you abandoned me?

And when they had heard this in the crowd, they started to laugh and said, "He is calling Elijah the prophet; let us see whether or not Elijah appears."

Then Jesus said, "Drink."

And one man took a sponge, doused it in vinegar (a bottle of it was standing nearby), stuck it on the end of a reed and offered it to Jesus.

Jesus sucked on the sponge and said in a loud voice, "It is done! Father, I offer my spirit into your hands."

And bowing his head, he surrendered his spirit.

Conclusion

THE FIRST EPISTLE OF JOHN
THE EVANGELIST

Jesus Christ's proclamation on goodness is a proclamation concerning the knowledge of life, under which knowledge people may have communion with the father of life and consequently have eternal life. This is a proclamation on true goodness.

The knowledge of life consists of knowing that God is life and goodness and that in life and goodness there is no death or evil. If we had said that we were united with God, but we live in evil and death, then we are either beguiling ourselves or are blatantly lying.

Only if we live the same sort of life that Jesus lived, only then can we be united with him. We ought to consider the life of Jesus Christ an example of true life. He saved us and the whole world from falsehood. Only he who recognizes Jesus's teaching and fulfills his commandments is a true Christian.

Whoever says that he recognizes Jesus Christ's teaching but does not fulfill his commandments is a blatant deceiver; there is no truth in him. And whoever fulfills his commandments will have love for his neighbor. Only through this love can we unite with God. Whoever says that he has united with Jesus Christ should live just as Jesus lived. Whoever says to himself that he exists in life and goodness but hates his living brother does not exist in life and goodness, but in death and evil, and doesn't know himself what he is

THE GOSPEL IN BRIEF
doing. And whoever hates the life that is within him is a blind man.

In order to not be a blind man, one must remember that all things worldly and earthbound are lusts of the flesh or are vanity, and none of this comes from God, that all things worldly are transient and they die.

And only love and good deeds motivated by love are eternal.

Only he who recognizes his spirit as the son of the father, only he may unite with the father. And therefore, hold tight to this knowledge that in spirit you are the son of God the father. Having this surety, you will receive eternal life.

God gave us the opportunity to be his sons and the same as he himself is. And so we become his sons in this life. Although we do not know what will happen with us afterwards, we do know that we are the same as him and that we can unite with him.

Hope for this eternal life will save man from all errors and will make him pure, as pure as the father himself is. Everyone who does evil deeds acts against the father's will.

Jesus Christ appeared to us in order to teach us salvation from sins and communion with God. And therefore whoever has united with him can no longer sin. Only he who does not know him can sin. And whoever lives within God does what is right. Whoever has not united with God does not do what is right. Whoever has recognized his nativity from God can no longer commit lies. And therefore people can be divided into godly ones and ungodly ones, into those who know the truth and love their brothers and those who do not know the truth and do not love their brothers, because, according to Jesus Christ's proclamation, we cannot fail to love our brothers.

According to Jesus Christ's proclamation, we know that we will cross over from death into life if we can begin to love, and that whoever does not love his brother resides in death. We know that whoever does not love his living brother does not love life. And whoever does not love life cannot have life.

According to Jesus Christ's proclamation, we know that life is given to us out of love for us, and that therefore we should give our own lives out of love for our neighbor, that is, we should sacrifice our lives for the good of our neighbors. So whoever has life and sees that his brother is in need but does not give up his life for his brother has no godly love within him.

One should love not with words, but with deeds and with truth. And whoever loves in this manner will have a peaceful heart because he will be united with the father. If his heart struggles, then he will subdue his heart for God. Because God is more important than the desires of his heart. If, though, his heart does not struggle, then he is blessed. Because he is doing all that he can, the very best, and is fulfilling all that had been commanded him. And he is commanded to believe that he is a son of God and to love his brother.

Those who act in this manner unite themselves with God and become higher than the world, because what is within them is greater and more important than the whole world.

Therefore let us love one another. Love comes from God and everyone who loves is a son of God and knows God. And whoever does not love does not know God because God is love.

That God is love we can deduce from the fact that he sent his spirit, which is the same as him, into the world and gave us life through that spirit. We did not exist and we were not necessary to God, but he gave us life and goodness and accordingly, he loved us.

No one can fathom God. All that we can know of him is that he loved us and gave us life by means of this love. And therefore, in order for us to be in communion with God, we must be the same as he is and do the same as he does, that is, we must love other people. If we love one another, then God is within us and we will remain within him. Having understood God's love to us, we believe that God is love and that whoever loves is united with God. And having understood that, we do not fear death, because we have become the same as God, as far as this world is concerned. Our life has become love and we have been liberated from fear and all suffering.

We love because God loves us. And we do not love God, whom it is impossible to love, because no one can see him, but we love our brother, whom it is possible to love. Whoever says that he loves God, but hates his brother, is fooling himself because if he does not love his brother whom he can see, how can he love God, whom he cannot see? And so, we are given the command to love God since he resides within our brother.

God's love consists of fulfilling his commandments. And his commandments are not difficult for the one who, recognizing his nativity from God, becomes higher than the world. Our faith elevates us higher than the world. And our true faith is in the teaching of Jesus, the son of God. He taught us that there should not just be flesh alone, but also spirit.

And the spirit is within us and confirms in us the truth of his teaching. If we believe the things that people assert, then how can we not believe the things that the spirit within us asserts?

Whoever believes that the spirit of life is within him, the spirit that comes down from above, can experience satisfaction within himself. Whoever does not believe that his life is a spirit that comes from the father above makes God into a deceiver. The spirit confirms that the life within us is an eternal life.

Whoever believes that this spirit is the son of the eternal spirit and is the same as that spirit has eternal life. And for whoever believes this, there is no obstacle in life, and all that he desires, according to the will of the father, will all come to pass for him.

And therefore, whoever believes that he is a son of God does not

THE FIRST EPISTLE OF JOHN

live in falsehood but is purified from evil. Because he knows that the earthbound world is a delusion and knows that within himself, within man, there resides the intelligence capable of comprehending all that truly exists.

Only the spirit—the son of the father—truly exists.

VERSE INDEX

This index refers the reader to the specific chapters and verses from which Tolstoy's translation arises. The left column contains the title of the Gospel, with chapter and verse. The right column marks the beginning and ending of the corresponding text, with the ellipsis denoting all text included between the associated beginning and ending points.

INTRODUCTION

CHAPTER I

CHAPTER 2

CHAPTER 3

CHAPTER 6

CHAPTER 7

CHAPTER 8

CHAPTER 9

CHAPTER 10

CLASSIC WORKS BY LEO TOLSTOY

THE GOSPEL IN BRIEF
The Life of Jesus

ISBN 978-0-06-199345-9 (paperback)

The greatest novelist of all time retells "the greatest story ever told"—the life of Jesus Christ—integrating the four Gospels into a single, twelve-chapter narrative.

GREAT SHORT WORKS OF LEO TOLSTOY

ISBN 978-0-06-058697-3 (paperback)

Eight of Leo Tolstoy's brilliant short novels, collected and reprinted in one volume.

WAR AND PEACE
Original Version

ISBN 978-0-06-079888-8 (paperback)

The original edition of Russia's most famous novel, shorter and more narrative in its initial incarnation, with several intriguing differences in plot.

FAMILY HAPPINESS
Stories

ISBN 978-0-06-177373-0 (paperback)

Reprinted here are two of Tolstoy's finest short novels—*Family Happiness* and *Master and Man*—and one short story, *Alyosha the Pot*.